Celia Dodd has written extensively about family matters for newspapers and magazines, including *The Times*, the *Independent* and the *Radio Times*. She has experienced each stage of the empty nest herself.

'In *The Empty Nest* Celia Dodd reminds us that our children continue to need us, just as we continue to value our relationship with our now young adult sons and daughters. This book will guide us as we seek closeness without dependence or intrusiveness. A thoughtful and compassionate exploration of a complex parenting phase'
Terri Apter, author of *The Myth of Maturity: What Teenagers Need from Parents to Become Adults*

The Empty Nest

How to survive and stay
close to your adult child

CELIA DODD

piatkus

PIATKUS

First published in Great Britain in 2011 by Piatkus

Copyright © Celia Dodd 2011

The moral right of the author has been asserted.

A CIP catalogue record for this book
is available from the British Library.

ISBN 978-0-7499-5386-7

Typeset in Sabon by Palimpsest Book Production Limited,
Falkirk, Stirlingshire
Printed and bound in Great Britain by
CPI Mackays, Chatham ME5 8TD

Piatkus
An imprint of
Little, Brown Book Group
100 Victoria Embankment
London EC4Y 0DY

An Hachette UK Company
www.hachette.co.uk

www.piatkus.co.uk

To Tom, Paul, Adam and Alice

Contents

Acknowledgements

Above all, I would like to thank all the parents and young adults who agreed to be interviewed for this book and who expressed themselves so thoughtfully and articulately on what often proved to be a painful subject. They all brought fresh insights which not only informed the book but also helped me to cope with this challenging phase of parenting myself. I am also grateful to the psychologists and psychotherapists who were so generous with their time, particularly Dr Terri Apter, whose wise work on family relationships is essential reading for empty nest parents; Denise Knowles of Relate; Ruth Caleb of the Association for University and College Counselling; Professor Cary Cooper; Professor Harriet Gross; Professor Charles Lewis; Kate Daniels, John Hills, Judith Lask and Jan Parker of the Association for Family Therapy and Systemic Practice.

I would also like to thank Hilary Arnold, Emma Dally and Kate Mosse for their advice, Natacha Ledwidge for inspiration and empathy, and Deborah Barker for regular injections of energy and insight. Finally, this book would not exist without the support of my agent, Laura Longrigg, Anne Lawrance, Claudia Dyer and all the team at Piatkus, including the copy editor, Jan Cutler.

Introduction

'The empty nest isn't just about the pain I felt when the kids left. It's the end of an era, a turning point in your life when you have to make big decisions about the future and renegotiate your relationships.'

Clare, whose son and daughter have both left home

The driving force behind this book came from meeting parents who felt as sad as I did about their children leaving, yet found no comfort in outdated stereotypes of empty nest syndrome which bear little relation to parents' lives today. A feeling persists that only a certain type of traditional housewife is affected, and that modern women who are used to more control and more choice would be immune. Where does this leave mothers – and increasingly fathers – who are devastated when their children leave, whether they work or not? Many feel isolated and in need of reassurance and support.

It's almost as if a taboo exists: talking about how much you miss your kids is on a par with discussing hot flushes. Yet there is huge comfort in hearing other parents talk about their experiences, and in this book 40 mothers, fathers and young adults talk frankly about the empty nest. Their voices are illuminated by leading psychologists and psychotherapists in the field.

This book is not just about missing your children and

learning to live without them. It is also about building a new relationship with your children as they grow into adult independence. The chapters are divided into the three key strands which face all parents: facing loss, establishing an enduring relationship with the departing child, and making the most of freedom by forging your own new direction.

The years when kids start taking their first steps in the wider world, often with one foot still in the family home, set the tone of the relationship between parents and offspring in the years ahead. Get things right now and parents stand a good chance of establishing a strong, lasting relationship with adult children who will visit because they want to, not out of duty. Yet while parents are bombarded with advice when their kids are young, it is thin on the ground during this most important and challenging phase of parenting. 'At no time in the life of a parent is listening and picking up on cues more important. At no time in the life of a parent is understanding a daughter or son more difficult,' writes the psychologist, Terri Apter, senior tutor at Newnham College, Cambridge.

Meanwhile, there are extra challenges for the current generation of parents; the empty nest is a very different experience for us than it was for our parents. Since we left home ourselves there has been a revolution in family life, and particularly in women's lives. Working mothers, 'New Dads', the rise in single-parent families, and the new closeness – almost friendship – between the generations have all had a huge impact. This generation of working mothers, accustomed to a degree of control over their lives, can be taken aback by the unexpectedness of this emotional upheaval.

Clare is one of the mothers I interviewed who least expected to be affected when her son and daughter left; she had a fulfilling career, a good marriage and plenty of interests beyond the family. She says, 'The empty nest isn't just about the pain I felt when the kids left. It's the end of an era, a turning point in your life when you have to make big decisions about the future and renegotiate your relationships.'

At its heart lies the identity crisis that confronts empty nesters whatever their circumstances. It is the flipside of the seismic emotional adjustment that new parents go through with the birth of their first baby. A return to life without children – while still being a parent – requires another massive readjustment to your sense of self and your place in the world.

On the whole, the empty nest is still tougher for mothers than for fathers, and not just because of the powerful biological connection that goes back to the womb. When the bond is broken, or at least stretched, it is no coincidence that women describe their reaction in very physical terms; a hand often goes to the heart as they speak. Some women even experience physical symptoms, while an expression of emptiness is almost universal. Clare says,

'When Sam went on his gap year I felt a sort of hollow; a part of me wasn't full any more. I think the emptiness I feel is to do with the physical closeness of your child, who's been with you since the womb. I remember when I was pregnant thinking this is amazing, there's this little being who is with me all the time; I'm not alone. It's a connection, like a cord of love that binds you to your child. When they go away it feels as if parts of it have been severed but it's still connected. It feels quite visceral.'

On a practical level too, mothers' lives are more closely interlaced with their children's than most fathers. Whether or not they work it is generally mothers who organise their own routines around the kids, deal with the nitty-gritty of their children's lives, sort the socks and pick up the emotional pieces.

As fathers become more involved with their children's upbringing, however, the more likely they are to face a parallel identity crisis. Chapter 4 is devoted to fathers, and their experiences are featured throughout this book. It is surely significant that some of the most moving accounts of children leaving home are written by men, including the former Poet Laureate, Cecil Day-Lewis, the playwright Jack Rosenthal (late husband of the actress Maureen Lipman) and the award-winning novelist J. G. Ballard. In his auto-biography, *Miracles of Life: Shanghai to Shepperton*, Ballard wrote: 'But childhood has gone, and in the silence one stares at the empty whisky bottles in the pantry and wonders if any number of drinks will fill the void.'

Because parents generally feel closer to their children than they were to their own parents, they dread them leaving even more. Letting go of your child and establishing an adult relationship becomes a more complicated affair, particularly thanks to the trend that sees adult children continuing to be dependent well into their twenties. It is even harder if adult kids boomerang back to live at home, as one in four men and one in six women now do.

The idea that it is vital to cut the apron strings persists, and parents worry that by supporting adult children we are somehow holding them back. After all, legal parental respon-sibility ends at 18, the official age of maturity. It doesn't help that parents tend to romanticise the way we left home back in the 1960s and 1970s. Most of us sound rather proud that we couldn't wait to leave home and never looked back, and applaud our own youthful independence and willingness to thrive in squalor. Yet it's a mixed message, because at the same time many parents don't want their kids to go and are secretly thrilled by their continuing dependency.

Perhaps now that we are parents ourselves the boomerang phenomenon will lead to a wider questioning of our attitudes to independence and a comparison with other cultures, where families aren't so stuck on the idea that healthy development requires separation and the pursuit of individuality. John Hills, Vice-Chair of the Association for Family Therapy and Systemic Practice, says, 'In other cultures kids stay at home well into their twenties and even thirties. It is our Western cultural norm that says children ought to leave by the time they are 21. Actually there is no right or wrong; context is everything.'

This book is not just for families whose kids go to university – many of the parents interviewed had children who plunged straight into work and adult life. It is more of a shock if the nest empties overnight, either because your young adult bypasses higher education or is an only child. The more children there are in a family and the wider the age gap between siblings, the longer the nest takes to empty, with several stages of coming and going before everyone leaves for good. The university years wean parents off more gently, but the fundamental emotions and challenges are the same.

For couples, one of the biggest concerns is whether their own relationship will survive without the common bond of childrearing. It is surely no coincidence that divorce rates among the over-50s have risen sharply in the last decade – often relationships which have hung by a thread of raising children together. Even apparently solid couples get shaken up by the transition. But there is good reason to be optimistic: recent research from the University of California found that, contrary to popular myth, many marriages improve when children leave home.

Again, social change has had an impact. Women are no longer expected to fit their lives around their husbands' plans, and often they are more likely than their partners to want to forge ahead with interests and careers that were put on hold while they brought up the children. For many couples such strong separate interests and identities, backed up by their shared history as parents, are an enduring source of strength. But implicit in the empty nest is the choice to stay or go, and inevitably some couples decide to part.

Parents are under extra pressure if parallel transitions overlap, notably the menopause and ageing or dying parents. Yet, mothers and fathers have a huge, hard-won advantage when it comes to surviving the empty nest: adaptability. Twenty-plus years of constantly reacting to the vicissitudes and crises of family life have taught us to be flexible and endlessly inventive. And there are positive reasons why the empty nest, like any change, is painful: because it involves such a radical reassessment of one's role, both as a parent and as an individual, it has great potential to be a positive phase of new beginnings and personal growth. There is a new urgency as suddenly the next stage – grandparenthood and retirement – doesn't seem so far away.

Finally, when Chloe, a stay-at-home mother with three daughters, read through her own quotes for this book she said,

'It makes me realise how isolated I am actually feeling and I am heartened to think that there are other parents out there working it out too. Most of my friends have younger children and I miss having peers to keep me in balance and say it's all OK. I would love an older mentor to say, "I remember going through this, keep going, you're on the right track, don't feel you've failed because you're asking all these questions."'

I wrote this book while experiencing each stage of the empty nest myself, as my two sons and daughter left home. The voices of all the parents I interviewed, including Chloe's, have acted as a kind of mentor for me. They continue to be a huge support in getting me through my darkest hours as well as an inspiration in optimistic moments. I really hope their voices will do the same for other parents.

PART 1

Facing Up to Loss

Chapter 1

Preparing to Part

'Your children are not your children.
They are the sons and daughters of Life's longing
for itself.'

The Prophet by Kahlil Gibran

Preparing for the empty nest is the key to surviving it. Thinking ahead and making plans for a future without children can make parting less painful. At the same time it is important not to lose sight of the present and to make the most of the time you have left together.

Almost as soon as children are born they start developing separate, if parallel, lives. It is such a gradual process that parents barely notice it happening until they hit a milestone that makes them sit up and take stock. It gathers serious momentum in the final years before kids leave, when many parents are struck by a moment of poignant recognition. The family therapist, Jan Parker, has three teenage children, including twins on the brink of a gap year. She says, 'From the point when I really acknowledged my children leaving home, when it changed from a known but distant reality to something approaching on the horizon, time began to race. It was a real bittersweet agony. I can feel time slipping away and I have to stop myself being irritatingly overly attentive. I can already feel myself trying to prepare.'

*   *   *

Many parents go through the final year or two with a creeping dread, which they keep firmly under wraps for fear of laying it on their kids. The prospect of life without children is unknown territory, and it is impossible to imagine how it will feel. This is the time to think about the various ways life will change: how your own life will be different, and how your relationship with your child will move forward. It is also an ideal opportunity to prepare your child to be more independent: you will feel a lot better when they go if they are ready and able to cope without you.

Growing apart together

Milestones, like learning to ride a bike, the first day at school or the first trip away, are just as significant for parents as they are for children, because they are poignant tasters of a future without them. Perhaps for the first time child and parent have conflicting reactions: the child's pride in their achievement is unambiguous; a parent's pride is tinged with the slightest sense of foreboding.

Heather says,

'Ever since my daughter was born I've dreaded her leaving home and wondered how I will cope without her. When she was six she asked if she could visit her aunt in Brighton, which meant going on the plane on her own. When she took the air hostess's hand at Edinburgh Airport she was so excited she forgot to say goodbye. I felt this awful wrench, but there was something about how confident and happy she was about going that made it bearable. I felt the same when she was a teenager and went away on her own for a fortnight for the first time. You think, how will I ever cope with my beautiful daughter getting on a train and arriving in a strange city on her own – you think of all the terrible things that could happen. But at every transition she has been so ready to go, and when the time came it was always fine.'

By jolting parents into a vision of the future each bittersweet transition helps them to prepare one step at a time. 'Parents have their transitions just as children have theirs,' says Ruth Caleb, former Chair of the Association for University and College Counselling. 'When children start school we begin to lose that very close relationship where we know everything about them on a day-to-day basis, and by the time they are at secondary school we may not know a lot about their lives. Each transition ought to be an opportunity for parents to ask, "What does this give me space for now? What am I going to do with this?" And always preparing yourself for the fact that you don't own your children, they will move on, but that doesn't mean that they will move away from you emotionally.'

Awareness of the growing separation intensifies in the teenage years. A new physical and emotional distance is common around the time children start secondary school, and spend most of their spare time in their bedrooms rather than mucking in with the rest of the family. Even the most physically demonstrative children turn into teenagers who shrug off hugs and demonstrations of affection. Suddenly the intimacy parents took for granted with younger children feels as if it is gone for good. Teenage boys notoriously shrink from their parents' – and particularly their mothers' – touch. It makes the prospect of saying goodbye even harder. If parents could see the future, and that when kids are really grown up they are happy to hug you, they might not feel so sad. The first boyfriend or girlfriend often increases the distance.

Thinking ahead helps

The sixth-form years are the ideal time to prepare for the future. There are three main areas of life that will be affected:

- How your own life will change.
- How your child will manage without you.
- How the bond between you will change – now is the time to think about how the relationship can be nurtured.

How your life will change: preparing for freedom

The huge benefit of anticipating the ways daily routines will change, and even starting new activities that have nothing to do with the family, is that it gives you a very positive sense of looking forward rather than back. Without careful fore-thought there is a danger that the exciting potential of all that precious extra time will get swallowed up in longer hours at work or by boring chores that expand to fill whatever vacuum opens up. Thinking ahead will allow you to hit the ground running as soon as the kids leave. But there is no pressure: many parents need a breathing space, a kind of sabbatical, after their kids have gone, before they can actually implement change.

Every parent feels differently about the prospect of their children going: many dread it, while others almost relish the idea – particularly women who started their families young, or who have several children and have been parenting without a break for years.

Case Study: Philippa and Monica

Philippa was 22 when the eldest of her three children was born and is about to say goodbye to her youngest. Now in her mid-fifties she is cautiously optimistic:

'I'm quite looking forward to the next phase of my life, when it can be more about the choices that I want to make and not the adjustments I've got to make to accommodate my children. That sounds callous, but I've never experienced adult life without children. I've never come home from work and only had myself to think about.'

By contrast, Monica, a single parent whose only child was born when Monica was in her late thirties, dreaded her daughter going:

'In the years before Asha left I would lie awake at night in a state of fear and think, *Oh my God!* But I didn't do a lot to prepare except angst about it; I found it really difficult to make plans for myself. All I knew was that I had to go out more, because the very comfortable pattern I had got into was going to end – of being tired when I came home from work and knowing Asha was going to be there and being able to cook for her, watch telly together and chew over the day.

'I was aware that I'd got into a habit which was very limited. So just before she left, after worrying and worrying about it, I finally made plans. I arranged to go out more with my mates in the weeks after she left. Most significantly, I managed to fulfil a long-held dream by booking, last-minute, a place on a garden-design course one evening a week. Quickly I discovered that if I made the slightest effort I could be busy the whole time. That helped me to think more positively about the future and actively look at alternatives to living on my own.'

Breaking habits

The year before kids leave is a good opportunity to work towards breaking habits and routines. Mothers get so used to rushing home to cook, or never making plans for themselves on those days when the kids need lifts, that it takes a leap of imagination to picture a life with fewer demands. And it can be unsettling. Philippa is well aware that routines that have lasted years may be a comfortable excuse for not doing other things:

'My husband keeps telling me to get out of this idea that I have to cook a meal every evening, because in a few months James is going to have to sort himself out. But I've created this narrative in my mind that I really enjoy cooking, although actually I'm not sure that's true. I know I'm going to have to let go of it, but what else am I going to do? There are rituals I've got to let go of and I am anxious about that. There are a lot of other things which are really important to me that I want to develop, but I worry whether I can find it within myself to pursue them when I'm given the opportunity. I fear that I will die before I do anything else apart from work hard and look after children. I'm quite preoccupied by the future because I really want to make the most of it.

'For years I kept work quite circumscribed, because I put the children first: I worked four days a week, left on the dot of five o'clock and never took work home. When James goes I could be in a really strong position to make a lot more of my career and I could work much longer hours. But I'm not sure if that's what I want, because there are so many other things I would like to do.'

Work

The vast majority of mothers, and increasing numbers of fathers, have, like Philippa, made compromises in their working lives to accommodate their children. With the empty nest the need to compromise falls away, and parents find themselves at a crossroads where they can reassess their working lives. It pays to think ahead and consider the options, because it can take months to find a new job, or change roles within a company, or to get new qualifications. Nina discovered this when she saw an advert for her ideal job volunteering at a medical organisation which required a Human Rights degree. It was the perfect spur to act: while one daughter was still at home she gave up one of her two part-time jobs and signed up for an MA.

Getting back to work

Many of the mothers I spoke to who had given up work to bring up children were particularly keen for a total change and enthusiastic about getting back to paid employment. It can be useful to test the waters by applying for jobs and investigating courses long before the children leave.

Case Study: Heather

Heather, who has devoted her energies full-time to home-educating her two daughters for 20 years, is gearing up for the particular challenges she will face when the younger one goes to college in a few months. She is already exploring various options, including a course run by her local council for people who have been unemployed for a while. She says,

> 'I feel really positive about the future, sometimes excited and sometimes a bit scared and unconfident. I got quite interested in a part-time supply teaching job, but they had been inundated with applications and although I am well qualified I realised I can't just glide back in. That gave me a glimpse of how it might feel next year. Now I want to step back and take time to think about what to do next.'

Heather has many options she could explore; in anticipation of the empty nest she set up children's sewing classes and started selling imported jewellery. But she is also keeping an open mind for totally new possibilities.

How to prepare for an uncertain future

The problem about making concrete plans for the empty nest is that parents can't be certain what the future holds. Before the children leave, parents dream about a future of uninterrupted free time and emotional space. But it rarely turns out quite like that, because children still need support, albeit at a distance. The Cambridge University psychologist, Terri Apter, advises parents to prepare for uncertainty and to stay flexible: 'It's difficult to plan ahead because you don't know what form the empty nest is going to take. Don't act on the assumption that you can now be totally me-based. Your children are still going to need you, but you don't know for how long and in what way. Often there are still many developmental glitches to come. A lot of parents say they were expecting the empty nest but find that it isn't empty, it's a revolving door as children come back home for a while, then leave – or come to a bifurcation in the path and just don't know what to do. You don't know what it's going to be like, and it's not your fault or your child's fault if something goes wrong.'

Preparing your child to manage without you

The empty nest will be more bearable for parents if they feel their children are ready to cope away from home both practically and emotionally. Yet teenagers may miss their parents' love and support more than they expect, and they are notoriously clueless about laundry and cooking. Ryan, 19, and in his first term at university, says, 'I'm getting quite worried about my diet. I chose self-catered accommodation because I thought the food would be horrible but I don't have time to think about eating healthily. You can buy three frozen pizzas for a fiver, so that's all I've eaten this week.'

University counsellor, Ruth Caleb, says students' lack of domestic nous is an increasing problem for universities: 'I've seen how distressed students become when they don't know how to look after themselves. It's important that parents help their child become independent by encouraging them to take a more adult part in family life, for example by helping preparing a meal a couple of nights a week and doing their own washing. Nurturing a sense of responsibility will help them grow up in a way that makes it easier for both parents and children to let go, and welcome them back as young adults.'

Some experts recommend parents give kids their own special jobs from as young as two, and I have come across teenagers who happily help with housework – OK, not that many. While it clearly benefits everyone if domestic skills are absorbed as a natural part of daily life, many parents find it quicker and less bother to do it themselves; they can't face another argument and their kids need to focus on exams. In my experience, kids learn all this practical stuff when they have to, and if they show an interest in the year before they leave it's a perfect opportunity to pass on a few tips.

It is equally important not to be panicked into last-minute instructions, which simply add to the stress. It is impossible, as well as undesirable, to equip your children for all eventualities. What matters is that they know how to ask for help and that they also feel able to come back to you and ask. Alice, 23, says,

'I was better prepared than a lot of people in that I knew how to cook the basics and washing is common sense. It helped that I had visited my older sister at university, which gave me a sense of what it would be like not to be a child living at home with your parents. But I knew a lot of people, usually guys, who were rubbish at looking after themselves. They adapted quite quickly; you learn from other people and seeing how they cope.'

Decisions about careers and courses

Most parents naturally want to have a say in their child's choice of university, and most teenagers appreciate their input. Jo, 25, says,

> 'I wish someone had told me to think more carefully about which uni to go to, and that the place really matters as much as the course. I had this worry that although the course was perfect the city seemed so boring, but everyone said it would be fine. I hated it. I thought about leaving in my first year and I knew my parents would support me either way, but ultimately I felt they knew best. So I didn't leave, but I kind of wish I had.'

Parents tread a fine line between helpful involvement and being too controlling. Research by the *Times Higher Education Supplement* found that parents are increasingly involved with their children's choice of university; some even want to sit in on the interview. Parents' interest and involvement is natural and generally a good thing. But nobody would want parents to dissuade their children from a particular course or university. The final decision has to be the student's. Sarah, who has a son and a daughter at university, says,

> 'My kids think I'm a control freak, and I suppose I have interfered a bit, but I'm just trying to give them the benefit of my experience. They don't see it as good advice; they see it as me trying to control their lives. The more I nagged Kiran about applying to Oxford the more irate he got. I realised that if I forced the issue, and he got in and hated it, that would be much worse – and it would all be my fault. With Jasmine I tried to lay down the law and force her to choose a better career option than drama, but she was adamant. We had arguments where she accused me of

being unsupportive, but we finally arrived at a compromise: a combined degree.'

Young adults have equally strong ideas about university accommodation, which seems hard since parents are usually footing the bill. It can be a bone of contention, because it is hard to step back if they are dead set on self-catering yet are hopeless at cooking or remembering to eat and unrealistic about how much time shopping and cooking can take.

TIPS
Basics that adult kids need to know

Money
Young adults need to learn how to budget and have a rough idea of the cost of basics like coffee and fruit. Helping with the family's weekly shop, or even doing some of it themselves, will help. An independent attitude to money will gradually develop if teenagers are allowed to make their own mistakes with a weekly or monthly allowance.

Health
Encourage 17 to 18-year-olds to make their own doctor's and dentist's appointments and pick up their own prescriptions.

Sex
Each family has its own attitudes: some parents are more open about sex than others. Young adults often act as if they know it all, and get embarrassed and dismissive if parents try to broach the subject. If that is the case, and you worry that your child is not fully clued up about contraception, safe sex and the risks of

sexually transmitted diseases, give them a good book (see Resources) or ask your GP or practice nurse to have a chat with them. But it has to be up to parents to impart the most important information: about emotions, feeling ready for sex and confident enough to say no.

Drugs and alcohol

Again, different families take a different line on what is acceptable, and some are more liberal than others. Either way, parents hope their influence will persist in the face of peer pressure, and that is more likely if they have allowed teenagers to manage their own boundaries in an increasingly adult way. University counsellor Ruth Caleb explains: 'Teenagers still need boundaries, but boundaries need to change as parents recognise the child's budding adulthood. Teenagers have to learn to negotiate, yet some parents find this hard: at one extreme they may allow the child to do absolutely anything, so the child has no boundaries, and as a result, no sense of being cared for. At the other extreme parents may be intransigent and the child has no power at all. When those children leave home they often fail to manage their own boundaries – drinking far too much, taking drugs and getting behind in their studies.'

Food

It's important your child knows how to cook the food they like eating if they are moving into a flat or going for self-catered accommodation. Compile a personal cookbook of their most easily prepared favourite meals to take with them – if you're feeling arty it could even be illustrated with magazine pictures or family photos. Or buy them a cookbook aimed at beginners – illustrations are essential. Kids also need to know about basic hygiene and food safety, such as washing knives and chopping boards after contact with meat, and which foods need to be kept in the fridge, what must not be cooked from frozen and how long to reheat leftovers.

Laundry
Sort through your child's laundry with them and explain washing symbols and separating whites from colours and delicates from jeans. Explain what needs hand-washing and how to do it, what can go in the dryer and what needs hanging out. Give a rough idea how often they should wash bedding and towels.

Safety
Explain how to avoid electric shocks – very important with guitar players – why not to put metal knives in toasters or metal in microwaves, how to change a plug, that water and electricity don't mix, and so on. If they are taking a bicycle, go with them to choose a helmet and make sure they know the risks of not wearing it.

Cleaning
Run through a simple list of which products to use and how.

Personal safety
You are likely to get a better response if you share your anxieties rather than laying down the law. Even if young adults won't admit it, they probably feel a bit appre-hensive about staying safe on new territory. Be honest about what worries you, and explain that while you may be over-anxious that's part of your job as a parent, and discuss what could make you feel better. If you are calm, honest – and avoid referring to horror stories you've been told or read in the paper – it should sink in, even if they roll their eyes!

How the bond with your child will change: laying foundations for a new relationship

In the last few years at home the relationship between parent and child moves towards a more equal footing, a coming back together. Parents can promote this by a discreet change in the relationship in the sixth form years, seeing their children as equals in the house and generally giving them more responsibility. This move towards a close, enduring connection is a far cry from the once fashionable theory first mooted by the psychoanalyst, Anna Freud, who insisted that teenagers had to separate from their parents in order to establish their own relationships. Cambridge University psychologist, Terri Apter, believes this is unhelpful to parents and children. 'Anna Freud called adolescence a psychological version of parent–child divorce and she thought separation was absolutely necessary. Other psychologists have developed this to say that in order to be able to relate to their peer world, to be able to be intimate with someone else, teenagers really need to be psychologically independent from their parents' values, from their idealisation and love of their parents. This idea values independence and downgrades connection. In fact we are born into relationships of love and care, we continue to develop within these relationships, we change and update these relationships but we don't sever them.'

If parents are to offer appropriate support, Dr Apter believes they need to educate themselves about their children's worlds. This is not just about tuning into their tastes, but about making an imaginative leap into what life is really like for them. 'It's good if this starts in the late teens,' she says. 'Sit back and think, what is it like for them? You see them as young and having the world and every opportunity ahead of them, and in many ways they are very savvy. But how are they experiencing it? Just try to find out from them and try to avoid being judgmental.'

Practical ways to stay close

It can take an effort to connect with teenagers even when they're living in the same house: they're always out or in their room; everyone is busy. Teenagers invariably want a chat when their parents are shattered or there's a fabulous film on the telly. Liz, a single parent of four children, says,

> 'Sometimes teenagers feel like talking just when you're really busy, and you have to stop everything. With the older three, because I didn't work full-time, I was always around for those moments when they wanted a two-hour conversation, having said not very much for weeks. At times I would have liked to have not been working while Will is still at home – because if you're working then you are often not there when they happen to want to talk. It doesn't matter what it's about, it's just that they want to talk. I miss that.'

Yet, many parents wrongly assume their teenagers don't want to spend time with them. The family therapist, Jan Parker, says, 'Our children don't need us any less, they just need us differently. Teenagers tell researchers that they neither need nor want their relationships with their parents to become distant, but different. They want us to acknowledge, respect and adapt to their growing abilities and the changes they are experiencing.' Single mother, Liz, made a conscious effort to build on common ground with her teenagers, although it can't have been easy organising things around her part-time job and her other children, including Laura, who has Down's Syndrome. 'With the boys in particular I thought if I didn't take Will to rugby every Sunday or drive Jack to mountain-boarding competitions they would have a completely different life from me. So I've kept close to them, because I got involved with their interests when they were teenagers. They don't have to talk to me, but they do need to know I'm interested.'

Trashing the nest: conflict

Hopefully, the battles which often characterise the middle teenage years calm down in the period before children leave. But while many teenagers draw closer to their families as the parting looms closer, others distance themselves by being stroppy and uncommunicative. Uncertainty about the future can create conflict in the months before parting, when both sides are apprehensive about what happens next. One mother said she felt her son had to trash the nest in order to feel able to leave it.

Parents generally interpret stroppiness as a sign that the teenager is eager to leave, but it may be just the opposite: anxiety about leaving home and leaving childhood behind. This makes sense to Elizabeth, who looks back on a difficult final year with her elder son Oliver, who is now 24.

Case Study: Elizabeth and Oliver

Oliver left school abruptly before A levels and stayed at home for a year before getting a job and moving into his own flat. At one point he refused to speak to his mother, Elizabeth, who is a single parent with another younger son, for six months. Elizabeth says:

'Now I think part of his anxiety about leaving home was leaving me, and part of being foul to me was to prove to himself that I could manage without him. I realised I had to be as steady as I could so that he would feel OK about leaving me, and I think that is peculiar to being a single parent. We had a massive argument about him taking responsibility for his choices. He spent the year in bed, and given that I work from home – a small, two-bedroom flat – it was quite fraught. I came up with all sorts of suggestions – learn to drive, get a job, travel – but he didn't want to do any of them. He was a very cross, very

unhappy late-adolescent who felt really stuck. I could understand his huge frustration: he wanted to go out and conquer
the world but he didn't know how to begin. When he was
being mean to me he was actually feeling really unhappy
about himself and I was the only person he could risk
being mean to.'

The prospect of parting feels particularly sad because parents
have no way of knowing whether conflict and lack of communication will continue. John Hills, Vice-Chair of the Association for Family Therapy and Systemic Practice, is encouraging:
'Parents need to be open to the ambivalence, to the part of
the child that wants to stay as well as the part of the child
who seems to be saying, "I don't care how much I hurt you,
I'm out of here." The skilful parent looks beyond the conflict
and can see the vulnerability. Although it's a combative
façade, it conceals vast amounts of insecurity, doubt and
uncertainty, because it is a huge world out there and young
adults have no idea how to find their way in it. Parents
who have been through that phase themselves can connect
empathetically and keep a line of communication open
through the conflict. And if the understanding and connection
is right it re-engages later on.'

Gap years at home

Teenagers usually spend at least part of their gap year at
home, working to save money to travel and then when they
come home before university. Initially, parents may be thrilled
by the prospect of putting off the final departure and having
another year together, but the reality can be quite stressful.
The absence of school routines and terms offer the no-tabs
existence that teenagers crave, but parents are left floun-
dering, unsure which boundaries are still acceptable. Teenagers want a new adult status, but to parents they are still
recent school-leavers.

Philippa says about her experience of gap years,

'James asked us to just sort of ignore him, to behave as if he wasn't here; he wanted to do his own thing. I understand that he wants a change in the status of his relationship with us but if you're living with somebody in a family you can't really function like that. I still cook for him and I still ask where he's going. I can't sleep properly until I know he's back. I still feel tense about it whereas I feel my daughter, who has already left, has gone beyond the point where I'm monitoring her. It's hard to switch that off, although I wish I could.'

Sometimes, home-based gap years feel like an unnecessary extension of childhood. Parents who were happy to cook and clean for kids when they were studying or working hard soon feel resentful if they come home to find them lying on the sofa surrounded by ash trays and cereal bowls. But they are also good practice for the future, when adult children almost inevitably boomerang back into the nest. Janet found that her daughter's gap year, and her subsequent postgraduate moves back home, inspired conflicting emotions.

'Susannah and I had a slightly fractious relationship that year; I felt irritable and edgy. It was more about me than her. A lot of it turned on me wanting her to spend more social time with us, and me wanting more from her than she was reasonably able to give. There was this constant awareness that she would soon be going off, and that although this was still her home it was only for want of an alternative base. It's still true to some extent, but in that year before she went to university I was exceedingly conscious of it. Both our children are quite social beings, and it's difficult to fit in the parents at times!'

Relations can get even more strained when children come back from their travels. The initial thrill of meeting your child at the airport soon wears off as world-weary teenagers shoehorn themselves back into family life. They have developed their own strong opinions, agendas and body clocks, which may be totally at odds with the family's. Stories of kids cooking up all the food that was meant for supper at three in the afternoon and having noisy late-night gatherings are pretty standard. Meanwhile, they have had a taste of a different way of life, which can make them hypercritical of the way things are done at home. Beth remembers,

'Our eldest daughter, Daisy, could be a bit annoying in her gap year. She kept buying frightfully posh cookbooks and saying, "This is how we should be cooking Mum, not rice and dhal, we should be using organic cocoa." It really made me feel that it was time she had her own home, that she was ready to deal with the consequences of her own choices instead of feeling bound with ours. Basically, it felt like time for us to separate; her living here couldn't have gone on much longer, although we are still incredibly close.'

The final countdown

It's a cruel irony that in the final weeks before children leave, parents and kids often feel so stressed that it's impossible to enjoy precious time together. Anxiety about parting and how you'll handle it, coupled with time-consuming practical matters like sorting out finances and buying duvet covers, can be a stressful mix. It's probably easier to simply resign yourself to feeling a bit tetchy.

It always helps if parents can put themselves in their child's place and remember that they are probably apprehensive as well as excited about leaving old friends, whether they will find like-minded spirits and cope with the work. Monica remembers, 'On the last night, Asha was in floods of tears.

She was very frightened of not making friends and of missing home and the cat and me. I was very surprised by that; when I left home I was just so excited. It made it much easier for me because she needed to be cuddled and looked after on her last night.'

TIPS
Preparing yourself and your child

- Get into the habit of occasional weekends away: it will increase confidence (yours and theirs) about how your child copes without you, and how you cope without them. In some families this is standard, but other parents feel reluctant to leave teenagers alone, particularly when they will soon be gone for good, and some teenagers don't like it that much either. If so, keep it to one night, suggest they invite a friend, and leave clear instructions.

- Encourage your child to go away too. It's a good way to test the waters and nurture self-sufficiency.

- If they are going to university, suggest a visit to student friends or relations. It can really help to get a good feel for what student life is like.

- Prepare yourself by making plans: treats for the week after your child leaves, weekends away and long-term projects. Now is the time to investigate courses and evening classes.

Chapter 2

Facing the Empty Bedroom

'By 1980 my three children were adults and away at their universities. Within a year or two they would leave home and begin their careers apart from me, and the richest and most fulfilling period in my life would abruptly come to an end. I had already had a foretaste of this. As every parent knows, infancy and childhood seem to last for ever. Then adolescence arrives and promptly leaves on the next bus, and one is sharing the family home with likeable young adults who are more intelligent, better company and in many ways wiser than oneself. But childhood has gone, and in the silence one stares at the empty whisky bottles in the pantry and wonders if any number of drinks will fill the void.'

Miracles of Life: Shanghai to Shepperton by J. G. Ballard, who brought up his three children alone after his wife's death

Parents often say they can't bear to go into their child's bedroom because that is where they feel their absence most. It becomes a symbol of how parents feel in those early weeks when the sense of loss is at its most acute. Some empty nesters prefer to shut the bedroom door firmly for a couple of weeks, while others can't resist the temptation to sniff their children's clothes, even though it only makes them feel worse.

The empty nest has many stages, from the moment your first – perhaps your only – child leaves, to the time when all your kids have set up homes of their own (of which more in the next chapter). People often say things like, 'At least you've still got one child at home', but that misses the point, because the sense of loss is just as acute, even if only one child has left and there are others still living at home. Parting from each child is painful in its own particular way. What parents miss – mourn, some would say – is not so much 'the children' as the special relationship with each child. When he or she leaves home for the first time it feels momentous, whether they are the first to go or the last, and whether they are plunging straight into work, flying off on a gap year or starting university.

If you have only one child, it all happens in one fell swoop. If you have more than one child the nest empties more gradually; it's not so much that saying goodbye gets easier, but after the first goes at least you have more idea about what the future might hold, and you know that the relationship not only survives, but that it usually improves.

Sending a child off to university is very different from parting with one who leaves home to go straight off to work and live in their own flat. If they're going far away on a gap year it's different again. In some ways university is easier on parents because it weans you off gradually. Your home is still their home, they're generally still financially dependent, and because most kids come back in the holidays – at least at first – your life is still organised around academic terms.

At the same time, however, there is a finality about dropping your child at university, or at the airport, because there comes a point where you have to walk away, gulp and just let them get on with it. Patrick, who has twin sons – one who didn't go to university and one who did – remembers a difference in the partings:

'I vividly remember saying goodbye to Matthew when I drove him to university for the first time, because I had never experienced that with Matthew's twin, Paul, even though he had moved out first; this was something a bit more. Paul did everything young: he started work when he was 16 and moved in with his girlfriend and their baby when he was 19. So the contrast was quite great. Although they are twins, Matt has taken things more slowly, so his going away to university was very much part of a growing-up thing. It felt like much more of a watershed in his life and therefore in mine.'

If kids plunge straight into work and their own flat there is no such defining watershed. It's a swifter immersion into adult life, very different from the gentler transition of university, with no vacations for parents to look forward to. At the same time, if they live nearby – and at this stage young adults tend not to move far away – parents may be able to keep a weather eye on things in a low-key way, which just isn't possible if they are away at some distant university. For Elizabeth it was a relief that her son was nearby; he left school before taking A levels and after a fraught year at home moved in with friends when he was 19.

'Even though he's moved out all his stuff he is still quite a factor in my life. His flat is ten minutes' walk away and although he has an independent life he'll ring me up for help with things like taking rubbish to the dump, or to help take his cat to the vet. I feel he hasn't really left; he's still around – partly because he lives nearby and we have a much closer relationship now. I see him at least once a week – he comes round for supper one evening after work.'

Taking your child to university

Many parents dread the moment of parting for weeks, even months, and when it finally arrives they are not sure how to handle it. No matter how much you think you've prepared yourself, emotionally you can still be floored. There are so many conflicting feelings, both your own and your child's, to handle. They are excited, nervous, perhaps even tearful, and it's hard to keep track with how they want you to behave, because it changes constantly: one minute they want you to stick around, the next minute they are shooing you out of the door. The sheer effort of interpreting the signals and behaving accordingly can be draining. Sarah remembers,

'As soon as I left Kiran I burst into tears. I felt totally exhausted. It was such an effort holding in everything I was feeling about saying goodbye, and trying not to get upset, and at the same time second-guessing how he was feeling, and how he wanted me to behave. I was on my own, but I met up with another mother and we spent the rest of the afternoon in Starbucks crying and talking about our kids. That helped.'

Jenni drove her daughter to university with her ex-husband, and remembers,

'As we were about to leave, Rhiannon said, "Mum, I'm scared." I remember driving away feeling bereft, like I'd left something behind, a part of me. It made me think of her first day at school. I hadn't expected to miss her as much as I did. It was very intense, almost a physical ache, and it lasted months. Perhaps it's more intense because she's an only child and I'm a single parent.'

Saying goodbye is never quite what you expect. For some parents the months of anticipation turn out to be worse than the reality of parting, which almost comes as a relief. Some parents don't feel floored until a few days later. Others find that the full impact doesn't hit until they actually say goodbye. Charles Lewis, Professor of Family and Developmental Psychology at Lancaster University, says, 'I'm sure when many parents drive away after saying goodbye they park in a lay-by and dissolve in tears because the realisation of what parting actually feels like is so totally different from the anticipation. Beforehand we have all sorts of protective mechanisms which prevent us thinking about the disorientation and despair of not having our children with us. And when it actually happens there are real deep feelings of loss. One of the main ways of coping is to deflect those feelings. So, while you may burst into tears on the way home, by the end of the journey you are already beginning to resolve what to do next. You ring them when you get home and you gradually realise that although you won't see them for weeks there are other things to do.'

Your child's reaction

It is also impossible to predict how your child will react – and of course that is sure to have a huge effect on how parents feel when you leave them. Some kids meet new friends quickly and can't wait for their parents to leave, while others want them to stick around and help fix up their new room. Even confident children can be overcome by an attack of last-minute nerves when reality hits.

Rebecca, now 25, vividly remembers the shock of that first day six years ago.

'I remember feeling absolutely horrified, because I had spent so much time thinking about university and the whole process of actually getting there but I hadn't thought about what happened beyond that point. I was really excited because I'd always been told it would be the best time of my life, but at the same time I was a bit apprehensive and not sure I'd chosen the right course. I was horrified when my parents said they were leaving. I just sat in this empty room. I don't think I knew what I wanted. I think I was annoyed with them and upset that they'd left me, but I definitely wouldn't have wanted them to hang around because that would have looked so uncool. I just hadn't thought about the fact that I really was going to be on my own.'

Parents often feel racked with regret about what they did or didn't do. At the time it is so hard to know whether to stick around for a while, helping to make the room homely, or whether it's better to go quickly so that it's easier for your child to make friends without their embarrassing parents around. If you do that the chances are you'll soon start agonising about abandoning them. Martin still feels he made a big mistake when he dropped his eldest daughter, Daisy, at university, but how was he to know what to do? I must admit that when I took my own daughter to Edinburgh I took his experience to heart.

'It was disastrous. Five minutes after I left Daisy in her room she texted my wife Beth and said, "I want to die, it's awful." All her other flatmates seemed to have formed a common bond and she thought she was going to be rejected. Beth was really upset – she was worried that Daisy really did want to commit suicide or something. I felt this awful angst that I had done completely the wrong thing by taking her off for a walk through the city, finding her a bus timetable, and going to a local church. I felt terribly guilty that she had missed out on chatting with her new flatmates. But Beth talked to her and within about 24 hours it was all OK.'

Perhaps the best solution is to keep your options open. Give your child space to settle in and meet people, but stay nearby for a few hours, or even overnight, in case they need you; make sure they know you're available if they want you to pop back. One bonus is that this allows parents time to explore their child's new environs. Rose had contrasting experiences with her son, Jake, and her daughter, Maud, who left two years later. Jake wanted his parents to stay around for most of his first weekend, while Maud settled in instantly and just wanted to be left to get on with it.

'My partner and I took Jake to university. I think if both parents go it can make the child feel smaller in some way. Anyway he needed our support to ease him in more than Maud did. He wanted us to help find things for his room, so we took him out to dinner that night and stayed until the next morning. I went on my own with Maud, and I'd arranged to stay up there for a night because I thought she might be lonely and I would take her out to dinner. But as soon as I dropped her off I could see she would be OK: I remember thinking that she just knows how to behave at university in a way I never did. She texted me later saying, "Don't worry about dinner, I'm fine" – she'd met a group of people and was having a great time. So I was all on my own wandering around this strange city. I didn't mind at all, I was just relieved that she'd settled in so quickly.'

Tom and his wife took things a step further, by arranging a short walking holiday in the area after they dropped their daughter off; it meant they were able to check in on her a few days later, before they went home.

'It was a way of making a connection with the place – I felt I wanted to be part of where she was. My own parents never came to see where I lived when I left home and I regretted that, because I wanted them to know what I was doing. But perhaps Zoe thought we were being intrusive, looking at every nook and cranny of her room! I don't know. It was difficult driving away and leaving her. We kept putting off the final goodbye: it was, "Let's take you for breakfast", "Let's get you some books." We couldn't quite abandon her.'

It's even more difficult if you are anxious about how well your child will cope away from home and concerned that you might not have prepared them adequately. Sometimes concern is justified, sometimes it's not, but the best policy is to give your children the benefit of the doubt and trust them to manage. Suppress all the last-minute warnings that spring into your head about electric shocks and safe sex; write them down in a notebook and give it to them in a quiet moment if it makes you feel better (see the box on pages 19–21). Parents really can't prepare their children for every eventuality.

Judith Lask, Senior Lecturer in Family Therapy at King's College, London, says there may be underlying reasons why parents find saying goodbye particularly difficult: 'If you don't feel confident about your relationship with your child, you may worry about whether it will hold with this distance. Or there might be some vulnerability in your child, or they may have been in trouble in the past or had problems with drugs or whatever. Obviously a tremendous amount of extra anxiety will come piling in then – because once they've left you have responsibility without any control.'

Linda had a very good reason to be anxious, because her daughter, Madeleine, was diagnosed with cancer just before a gap year trip to Thailand. She started university just four days after she had finished chemotherapy and radiotherapy. Linda remembers,

'I was very concerned about her going, because I felt she was still very vulnerable. Her boyfriend and I drove down with her, and we were making her room nice – I'd bought a new bedspread and new towels, as you do – and she started to cry. It was just horrible. She was sitting howling as we unpacked her stuff. It was a terrible evening, with me trying to say it will all be wonderful. It was very hard leaving her on her own.'

Saying goodbye: is it OK to cry?

Opinions differ wildly about whether it's fair on your kids to cry when you say goodbye. Most mothers and some fathers selflessly draw on reserves of steely self-control to hold back the tears, because they don't want the departing child to feel bad or guilty. What makes parting so poignant is that while emotions run high on both sides, they are polar opposites: kids are excited, if apprehensive, while their parents are sad and anxious.

Phillip Hodson, Fellow of the British Association for Counselling and Psychotherapy, insists that it's fine to cry in front of the kids. 'If you're going to miss someone and you are tearful it is not going to burden your children; it means they know they are loved. But they'll probably be grateful to get out of your sight! You should never hide the way you feel; it's the only honest way to give information to the other person about the way the mind and the heart work.'

University counsellor, Ruth Caleb, has a rather different view. She is reluctant to be prescriptive about showing emotion, but ultimately she comes down on the side of self-control – partly, perhaps, because she is used to dealing with students in their first few weeks away from home. But, as a parent herself, she recognises how hard it can be to rein in your emotion: 'Leaving home to take your child to university for the first time is clearly a poignant shared moment for most parents and new students. However, when you say goodbye in their new "home" I think, if possible, you should try to leave them without your tears, because it's their day, not yours. Grit your teeth and cry in the car: don't let their last image of you be in a state. Leave with as much of a smile as you can muster and the sense that you know they're going to be able to do this. And make sure they know that you are there for them always. I put a little card with a message inside my son's case when he started university; it's a way of transferring your emotions. We were talking about it recently and he told me that when he opened it he burst into tears. He put it up on his wall and never took it down.'

A card in the case – or some other small token of affection – is a brilliant idea. I never did it myself because, even if I'd thought of it, I would have assumed my boys would have found it too soppy. Now that I've found out what other parents pop in the suitcase – letters, photos, their favourite choc bar – I wish I had, because this generation of kids seem to be more tolerant of parental cheesiness than we might expect.

It's one thing to shed a few tears or tell your child you will miss them; children probably rather like the idea of being missed. It is quite another to make them feel you are going to be lonely or miserable without them. Some children already feel slightly anxious about how their parents will cope when they've gone – sometimes with good reason – and most parents are keen to avoid behaving in a way that might add to this. Parents somehow need to manage their grief without overwhelming the child or making it their problem. For purely selfish reasons, letting them know too much about how bad you feel may be ultimately counter-productive because it may make them want to see you less, not more.

Family therapist, Judith Lask, says, 'While there is something good in your child knowing that this is an event for you, you should try very hard to manage anything that doesn't feel containable. You have to remember that for your child, however enthusiastic they are about moving out, there will also be a whole lot of anxieties about it as well. Also one of the things young people hate most is feeling guilty. One way of dealing with that is to totally avoid situations where they are going to feel guilty, which might be to have less contact with their parents, not more.'

TIPS
Saying goodbye

It can smooth the way emotionally if you sort out a few practicalities in advance and discuss what your child wants.

- Will both parents go, or just one? There are pros and cons to going on your own (or allowing your partner to go): it's easier to chat, or remain in companionable silence, if it's one to one, and it somehow feels more equal. And of course it may not be practical to leave younger children at home alone. But the journey home could be lonely.

- Some separated parents decide to send their child off together not just for the sake of the child but because it feels like such a significant moment which only they share.

- If only one parent is going, who will stay behind? It can be easier to hold back the tears if you know that the minute they've gone you can bawl your eyes out in private. But the big disadvantage is that you miss seeing how they've settled in and having a clear picture of their new environment, which can be a huge comfort in the weeks ahead.

- It is often a good idea to stay overnight nearby. The advantage is more time to help settle your child in – and you can pop back the next day to see how things are going.

- If you stay around, be prepared not to be needed – find out what films or plays are on that night in case they prefer to go out with their new friends. (Resist the temptation to drown your sorrows alone in your B&B).

- When you arrive, let your child get on with it: the first couple of days are when friendships are made (even if they don't last), and it can be easy for new students to feel they've missed some crucial bonding experience.

- Encourage them to make their bed first, before they do any unpacking, so if they come back exhausted they can fall straight into a comfortable bed.
- If you are leaving them at the airport, be kind to yourself. Don't prolong the agony by waiting for the last glimpse of that precious back: walk away purposefully and if you're upset, head to the loo and have a good sob before attempting the journey home.

Saying goodbye: gap years

Saying goodbye to a child who is flying off on a gap year is like any other goodbye but with knobs on. And there is something about airports that makes an already emotional parting even more highly charged. One minute you think you'll be hanging around for ages, but before you know it you're hugging them and they've gone. Even now, four years later, the image of that last glimpse of rucksack disappearing through the gate makes me well up.

It can be hard for kids too, although they may do their best not to show it. In her gap year Alice spent three months travelling around India on her own. Her mother didn't cry, but Alice certainly felt like it.

'My mum drove me to the airport; it was a night flight in January. I was completely terrified. I kept thinking, *What am I doing?* I didn't know anyone out there; I just had my backpack and nowhere booked. As I was saying goodbye I suddenly felt very vulnerable and I remember thinking, *This is the last thing I want to be doing right now, I just want to go home and wake up in my own bed tomorrow.* But while the process of getting there was really terrifying, once I was there I just had so much to think about. I had to adapt and take care of myself really suddenly, and it felt OK. I didn't feel my parents could do anything even if I wanted them to, so I just got on with it.'

Some parents hate the idea of a gap year because they feel their kids are too young to be wandering the world. Others like the prospect of delaying the final departure to university and the reprieve of a few months at home while kids save up. In fact, gap years can be particularly tough on parents, because it's a more drastic and more nerve-racking wrench than university. You don't just miss your child; you're worried about their safety so far from home and so far from caring adults. But with an estimated quarter of a million young Britons taking gap years every year, travelling is so much the norm that parents often go along with the idea until the trip looms large and reality hits home. Suddenly it feels like a very long time to be without them, and Thailand, or India, or Australia (the most popular destinations) seem terrifyingly remote. Teenagers who may never have been away for more than a couple of days now routinely travel to remote areas; kids who are used to being waited on hand and foot and being looked after when they get ill suddenly have to fend for themselves. Objectively, that sounds like no bad thing, but when it is your own precious teenager it can feel horrible.

Clare didn't expect to be upset when she saw her son off to the Far East; she had felt quite sanguine when her daughter left home and she was looking forward to having more time to pursue her own stuff. But when it came to the moment of parting she was devastated:

'I saw him off at the airport with his friend's mum and girlfriend, and when the boys went, the three of us were all in tears. Suddenly, five months just felt too long. Luckily the other mother was driving home, and because I was with her I had to be vaguely restrained until she dropped me off. I got back to an empty house – my husband was away working – and I just howled in the kitchen. I kept telling myself to get a grip on myself but I couldn't stop. After a while I thought, *That's extraordinary, that noise is me* – it sounded like a wolf calling. It was very surreal. Inside I was feeling this incredible pain and at the same time I heard this echoing noise.'

By contrast, when Judy's daughter walked through the departure gates at Heathrow, for a solo gap year in South America, Judy was apprehensive but remained dry-eyed. She had what she describes as an almost spiritual experience which took her totally by surprise because she is not usually that way inclined:

'I didn't feel sad when we took Haia to the airport. As I waved goodbye, my hand opened and I heard, in some way, really strong wings flapping. And I felt myself let her go as she disappeared through the gate. It was an incredibly emotional moment; an almost spiritual experience. I'm not prone to these things, but it felt very significant. I can't say that I totally let her go at that moment, because of course I carried on worrying about her. I loved having children and felt very lucky to have had four of my own and my stepson. But I was really aware of the timing and the role that I had in life changing. And I felt ready for it.'

Gap year anxiety

Gap year parents have to steel their nerves to face months of patchy communication and anxiety with little control. It is hard to remain rational even though you know there are all sorts of reasons why you can't get in touch: mobile signals are erratic; there is nowhere to charge up a phone and no Internet café. Parents just have to trust that their child has the gumption and common sense to cope and get over the feeling that it was only yesterday that they couldn't tie their own shoelaces. It is impossible not to worry when they ring up to say they're ill, or had an accident, or their travelling companion has abandoned them.

My second son's gap year kicked off with a teaching project in Swaziland – relatively reassuring – after which he planned to travel to Angola and Zimbabwe: terrifying. The realisation that we could no longer influence his decisions was hard. He wouldn't listen when we suggested that these might be slightly dodgy destinations, and I got used to waking up in the months before and during his travels with a gut-wrenching feeling of dread. But on balance it was worth all the angst. I've got a photo of Adam in Zimbabwe, which sums up how his gap year was for me. He's grinning with sheer pleasure on the top of a precipice, behind a sign saying 'Do Not Pass This Point'. It reminds me that despite all the anxiety I was glad that he was there, taking risks and having adventures without me there to hold him back by constantly saying 'Be careful!'

Like most parents, I also realised that the only way to stay sane was to focus my mind away from gap year horror stories and remind myself that the vast majority of kids come back in one piece, wiser and more appreciative of home. I did panic if I didn't hear from him for more than a couple of weeks, so I would just send an email shamelessly begging him to let me know he was OK. The days when he responded were flooded with sweet relief – the exception being the email that said he'd just cut his head open and a fellow worker had narrowly escaped an attempted rape. Mercifully, you don't hear about most of the bad stuff until they're safe and sound.

Facing the first weeks

In the immediate aftermath of parting it is hard to find anything good about your children leaving. In my darkest hours, nothing even comes close to cheering me up. Having a tidier house and less laundry seem hopelessly inadequate compensations for what has been lost, while freedom and extra time feel like a poor exchange. At this stage the very idea makes you feel more empty and lost. Psychologists and therapists agree on key strategies that can help parents get through those first few weeks when the sense of loss is most intense. They emphasise the importance of:

- Facing up to sadness
- Support
- Finding new occupations to fill the gap.

Facing up to sadness

Acknowledging how you feel, and accepting that you may feel sad for a while, is an essential first step. It's also important to recognise that, however inconsolable you feel, it will get better. The consensus is that while it is absolutely normal to be in tears a lot of the time for a week or so after your child has left home, if you are still in tears a month later it could be a worry. I always recover my equilibrium more quickly if I can have a good weep in private; it's miserable at the time but by the next day I'm getting back to an even keel.

Clare now looks back on the evening she spent howling hopelessly in the kitchen after her son flew off on his gap year as both necessary and therapeutic.

'There was something quite cathartic about letting it out; I think it helped, having a good old howl. Later that evening I went into Sam's room and had another tearful sad moment. I could still smell his smell and I kept thinking, *That's going to go soon.* But just before I went to bed I remember thinking, *I'm crying like this, but actually nothing awful has happened. It's totally natural, it's good that he's going off and being independent. And it's OK to be sad.* And then I had the thought that although he's not here any more he is on the same planet. He's also standing on the floor of the earth somewhere and we are still connected. It sounds ridiculous but somehow that gave me a huge boost, to think that we were still sharing the same air. I was still pretty weepy the next day but it did get easier as the days went by.'

Support

Many parents say they just get on with life, and it is not until they look back a few years down the line that they realise how deeply they were affected at the time, whereas others internalise their feelings, keep super-busy and push sadness to the back of their mind. Yet the right support from friends who have perhaps faced the empty nest themselves, or partners who are going through the same thing – albeit with a different response – can be hugely helpful. What parents need most is someone to acknowledge what they're going through, not just cheering up and reminding that their child will be home in a few months. Harriet Gross, Professor of Psychology at Lincoln University says, 'Most people want their feelings to be recognised as a genuine experience, and to be given time to express them and opportunities to think of ways through them – not just to be jollied out of it or dismissed by saying, "Let's go out for a meal" or whatever. The best way of being supported is not to be indulged, because that belittles what you're going through. What is needed is acknowledgement that recognises your feelings, moves you through it and enables you to go with it – and therefore makes it less of a challenge.'

Clare has been much more upset about her kids leaving than most of her friends, and their support helped her get through the difficult early days when her husband was away:

'The day after Sam left, a friend rang to see how I was and she could tell I was reluctant to go out or do anything, even though I was feeling lonely and sad. It was a sunny July evening and she brought wine and a picnic and we sat in the garden and just talked and even laughed. That did me good. Then she persuaded me to go to *Mamma Mia* with her the next day. That was the turning point. I was in floods of tears because it was such an unexpected affirmation of what I was going through. It was a huge comfort because it sums up the whole experience for me.'

Finding new occupations to fill the gap

At this early stage it can be hard to imagine that anything could take the place of children, and it requires a leap of faith to believe that eventually there will be compensations. Making plans and thinking about new projects helps, but if it feels too early, consolation can be found in familiar pastimes. Parents need to be gentle on themselves, and not be too worthy about the kind of activities they choose to fill the gap.

For the first couple of days after my kids leave I have learnt to be self-indulgent and please myself. I listen to radio dramas, knit, watch movies, drink tea and eat cake. I write my diary, look through old family photos, listen to cheesy tunes and think about how sad I feel. By the end of the weekend I'm over the worst and ready to plunge back into everyday life. And then they come home and you have to say goodbye all over again . . .

TIPS
When they first leave

- Indulge yourself by doing undemanding things you really enjoy, whether it's a manicure or a massage, meeting a friend for tea, buying flowers or going shopping. Soak in a bath, go to the movies, swim, bake a cake, update your iPod.

- It helps if you have already made a list of nice stuff to do, because when you're feeling inconsolable it's hard to think of anything other than wine and telly.
- Face your feelings. Look through old family albums and children's drawings, and have a good cry. Then phone a friend or do something fabulous.
- Find solace in music, films and books: *Shirley Valentine* by Willy Russell; *Mamma Mia* (especially that tear-jerking Meryl Streep number, 'Slipping Through My Fingers'); Joanna Trollope's *Second Honeymoon*; Cecil Day-Lewis's poem 'Walking Away'.
- Spend time with a friend you can rely on to be undemanding and genuinely supportive.

Chapter 3

The Nest Empties Completely

'While Charlotte remained, there was yet some distraction, some compensation for the absence of Peter . . . Only now, in the certain knowledge that, when next winter comes Charlotte will no longer be part of his household, does the loss of Peter, stretching into a future the duration of which no one can predict, feel intolerable.'

Music and Silence by Rose Tremain

Once the sadness of those first few weeks has begun to fade, life settles into a new rhythm. Parents now face a series of milestones, which are pretty clear-cut if children go to university, less obvious if they don't. If there is more than one child there is a further milestone, when all the kids go and the nest is completely empty. Emotionally it is rarely a straightforward progression from one milestone to the next; you don't just miss each child less and less as time goes on. One day you're ready to take on the world, the next you may be plunged back into misery and purposelessness.

The family therapist, Kate Daniels, says, 'We tend to think of progression through life as a single flowing stream, but it is actually very much forwards, back and stop, start. And once people accept that then it happens far less painfully. The whole process of getting over a child leaving home takes quite a while, because you have got to reorganise the whole basis upon which your life is predicated. It is a huge adjustment. It makes it a bit easier if you recognise that this is going to be hard, and you aren't necessarily going to "get over" it. Part of the problem these days is the tendency to foreshorten all our experiences, to believe that you can fix things quite quickly: my child's gone, I've just got to do certain things and I'll get over it. That is not how time organises us. So I think it helps if parents can think about it as a gradual process, and not to put pressure on themselves to try so hard to get over the child going.'

Every time you say goodbye . . .

You might think it would get easier to say goodbye, but sometimes it's even harder the second, third, and even fourth time. By now you know what life is like without your child, yet you probably won't steel yourself in quite the same way as you did when they first went. Monica, a single parent with one daughter, Asha, remembers,

'It was much worse when I took her back to art school after the Christmas holiday; it was like, "here we go again". I very rarely cry, but I burst into tears when I dropped her off. I was absolutely heartbroken. I drove off in tears, stopped to find a tissue and realised she'd left her phone in my car. So I had to turn round and drive back and found her in tears too. It was terrible having to say goodbye again; I was very upset.

'That second term without her was much harder than the first. I missed her support and her voice in my life and I was conscious that she didn't miss me in the same way, because she has so many new voices around her. Now my worry is what the empty nest will feel like when she has her own home and her own family – that is a whole different thing. And it feels quite scary.

'What surprised me was that right there with the sense of loss was a sense of relief. A burden was being taken off my shoulders. I had not faced up to just how stressful being a single parent had been, setting all the boundaries and rules with no partner to act as a counter, taking responsibility without support. Suddenly I wasn't worrying about when Asha was coming home and would she take a taxi and would she be in her bed in the morning? It felt like a real liberation.'

As time passes and parents get used to children's comings and goings you miss them a bit less. Every time you say goodbye it hurts again, but for most parents the initial sharp intensity of loss gradually fades into the new patterns of everyday life, only surfacing out of the blue when some random thing triggers a memory of how things used to be – the sight of toddlers on a beach, perhaps, or a joke you once would have shared, or passing the kids' primary school. 'Most of the time I don't miss the children at all, which makes me feel quite hard-hearted when I hear other women say how much they miss their kids,' says Amira. 'But occasionally I am overcome by a wave of sadness. In my mind's eye I can see myself walking hand in hand with my beautiful curly haired four-year-old boy. It's quite overwhelming – it's like grief. Because those children don't exist any more, it's almost as if they are dead.'

As time goes on, parents gradually get better at coping with poignant reminders and sad days. Parents who have already parted with older children have an advantage because they know how the relationship can develop in the future, whereas for parents facing separation with the first child it's pure guesswork. It has taken Clare two years to feel that she is over the worst. During that time she has worked hard on exploring the reasons for her grief and finding new ways of expressing her conflicting feelings. She says,

'I've got more used to Sam being away and I don't pine any more. It's easier to say goodbye now, but there is still sadness when he goes and I know I'll miss him. And I'm always thrilled when I know he's coming – my heart lifts.

He's got used to knowing he has to give me a very big hug when I see him! I definitely feel I'm making progress – although I still get pangs, especially when my husband is away. I still miss Sam and Charlotte and I miss being a mum. But the part which became empty when they moved out is filling up with other ways of nurturing myself and others.'

What if they don't come home?

Some kids come home too much; other kids don't come home much at all. This transitional stage between university and final departure can be tough for parents whose kids come home only for brief visits, even during vacations, and who send only the occasional text or email. It's even harder if your friends' kids keep in regular contact and come home frequently. For Anne, a designer and single parent of two children, the separation from her daughter, Jess, who started university two years ago, feels unexpectedly final.

'It was a shock how completely Jess left. It was like her life started as soon as she left home. Other parents tell tales of their kids always coming back at weekends, but Jess came back as little as possible and made very little contact, because she was having such a wonderful time. She deliberately went for accommodation which allowed her to stay at university in the holidays. I don't know why other parents' kids come home more; I don't know what other parents have done differently. It's not like I didn't cook all the meals and do all the washing – I did! I miss her very much. It made me realise that she really has gone and that I had to move on too. I miss that part of family life, and that she's not going to do things like come on family holidays. I don't talk to anyone about it; I think I've internalised it a lot. I think you just get on.'

But parents should not jump to conclusions about why their kids don't come home, because it might well be that they simply can't bear to tear themselves away from their new lives. Some psychologists even argue that it is the children who are most secure in their home base who are able to move furthest away. The family therapist, Judith Lask, says: 'Don't automatically construe their not coming home as not liking home. It doesn't necessarily mean they love you less; it might well mean that they feel quite secure and are just getting on with their lives. Remember that many parents wish their children wouldn't come home as much, because it means that they are not getting on and making friends.

'Having said that, your child's attachment history is important. Parents may feel the attachment their child has experienced with them is a bit insecure, because not everybody, for whatever reason, has been able to be a great parent. This may lead their child either to keep coming back more than they ought, or to go away and not come back because they have more of a disrupted attachment style.'

Whatever the reason, it is ultimately up to parents to keep the contact going. It's so easy to take umbrage if children don't return your calls, and to assume that they never want to speak to you. But that is almost certainly not the case, and there is no point sulking: parents have to be grown up and keep the lines of communication open without piling on the pressure. The occasional text or even a good old-fashioned letter is better than bombarding them with calls.

Some kids stay away because they feel guilty about not coming home more often – and, without realising it, parents make them feel worse. If kids stay away because they perceive their parents as too strict or controlling (or, as we see it, protective) there is not much parents can do, apart from accept that this is a painful but necessary stage in establishing the new adult relationship. Away from their parents' anxious gaze children are free to take risks, find out who they are, and grow up. The student perspective offers parents a few clues. Recently graduated Alice, 23, says, 'Most of my friends stayed in Manchester all the time; they saw it as home. It was partly that they couldn't handle going home to live with their parents, but mostly that they just didn't want to leave that bubble of student life behind.' Millie, 24, adds:

> 'If people didn't go home it wasn't so much because their parents were strict but because they came from boring places where there was nothing to do. I also had friends who only went home when they actually had to because they dreaded being stuck with their interfering mothers, or parents lecturing them and giving them a hard time. And I had another friend with a really needy mother: she hated going home because she had to face all the problems there, and the neediness of her family. Her mother would come up and bring loads of food just so she could see her. But she didn't stay long because her daughter clearly didn't want her to.'

University counsellor, Ruth Caleb, recognises how hard it can be for parents not to take it personally if their kids come home infrequently. Her wise words have certainly helped me through some of my darker moments: 'Knowing that people love you and are close to you is not about how often they come home. Love is not about seeing people all the time; it is about knowing you have a place in someone's heart, and that they have a place in yours. We all have the experience of a friend we rarely see but when we do see each other it is as if we've never been apart. The aim is to have that sort of close relationship with your child, where you don't need to be together all the time: your child knows how much you love and support them and neither of you needs to say so constantly or to be in touch every day. If the child seems happy and well, celebrate the fact that you have brought up an independent person who is able to make their way in the world, and that is a wonderful thing.'

When your child leaves for good

It is a huge milestone when your child leaves home for good to set up in their own place, whether it's a shared house, married bliss or a bachelor pad. It is this stage, when the children's departure is final, which many parents find hardest. Julia, who has two children in their thirties and two in their twenties, says,

'My youngest has just flown the nest yet again and maybe this time it's for good. It certainly feels like it and it is really rather strange: although he's been to university, this feels very final and quite sad. It's different again and perhaps even more challenging because of the realisation that both boys have finally left home to lead their own lives. When they were at university or even travelling afterwards, you knew they would come back, but now they really have left. This is yet another adjustment, which perhaps is the most difficult of all.'

Previous partings were sad too, but ultimately there was the consolation that they felt temporary, because the child was still based at home and probably not yet financially independent. This final parting is on another level, a much more defined separation. It's not only that your home is no longer their home. Your daily lives will never be intertwined in the same way again – not even in the holidays.

Case Study: Emma
Emma admits she was pretty blasé about the empty nest until her eldest daughter – she has three – left home for good. The nest has been completely empty since her youngest, Ruth, recently left on her gap year. She remembers,

'When Rebecca first moved into her own shared house it was a really strange, sad feeling that that was it; she wasn't going to be coming back. It hit me quite hard to think that there weren't going to be cosy family evenings in the way there had been in the past. It definitely felt more significant than when she and her sister went to university, because that felt temporary. I didn't feel sad at all then, and I didn't really miss them; it just seemed amazing that they were at that stage. I miss them much more now, which is funny – I find myself thinking that I haven't spoken to Rebecca or Alice for a few days. I miss our conversations. In fact she keeps in touch more than I do, because I don't like to intrude too much.

'Having a child five years younger than the other two means that we have been let into the empty nest gradually. A lot of our friends have two children close in age and for them it all happens so quickly. Now Ruth has gone it is very strange, being in this big house just the two of us. It's little things like not having to take the key out of the lock at night. And at first Ruth's radio still switched on automatically in the mornings, which made it feel even more strange that there was no Ruth around when I got up.'

Why some parents feel worse

Some parents find it much harder to cope than their friends, and are at a loss to understand why they feel so down. There are all sorts of obvious external circumstances which may conspire to make parents feel worse: if the rest of life isn't great, if other problems are getting you down, if you're worried about your child coping or about your relationship with them. If parents are divorced or separated, the anxiety that was felt during the initial separation might be rekindled: will my child find it more fun to be with the other parent and not want to come and see me? When the child leaves home the rhythm of contact which has developed over the years can get shaken up.

But leaving aside the wider context, there may be other,

more deeply rooted personal reasons which could explain why the separation is a much bigger blow for some parents than others. Even parents who seem to have everything in place to make the transition more bearable, such as a fulfilling career and a happy marriage, are often taken aback by the strength of their feelings.

Abandonment

The family therapist, Judith Lask, believes that the roots may lie in the patterns of attachment established in a parent's own childhood and youth, and that it is often people who find any change problematic who suffer the most. Some parents are unaware of having deep-seated feelings of abandonment until they are resurrected by an event such as the departure of a child. 'When a child leaves home you may find it triggers really deep anxieties from the past which make you feel pretty awful and scared. Even the most secure of us have felt insecure at some point, and any shock, or anything unusual which you have to negotiate, can revive those past experiences. So parents' individual attachment histories are really important, because the more secure you are the easier you will find it to negotiate changes like your child leaving home. If you have a secure attachment you feel far more confident that if people go away they will come back, and that you will manage on your own. You'll feel that even when you are apart you are still in their mind just as they are in yours.

'Parents' experiences of leaving home themselves are also important. If leaving home was a difficult time for you, if things changed in a negative way, or you floundered and were lonely, you will worry about your own children. If, on the other hand, it was a very exciting time, you will probably approach it with your children in a much more positive way.'

If you miss one child more

Some parents miss one child more than another, or get more upset when they go. It's certainly nothing to do with loving one child more than another. In fact, ironically, parents might find they miss the child they feel closest to least, because there is a sense of a continuing connection with children who keep in regular contact and are open about their lives. When the eldest leaves, it might feel like the hardest, simply because they are the first to go. When the middle one goes, there may be regret that you never had enough time on your own with them. And there is particular pain about the youngest going, because it's your baby and now the nest is completely empty.

Other factors influence how much you miss each child: the history of your relationship and what it's like now, as well as what's going on in your life. If you're worried about them, or they are having a hard time, they are bound to be even more in your thoughts. But if relations have been strained, the chances are that you will be relieved to wave goodbye to the conflict. Jackie admits that she missed her son much more than her daughter:

'It didn't feel sad when Hollie moved out because we had such terrible arguments in the last five years, which got worse when she started a business course and still lived at home. It was a huge relief to no longer feel like we were walking on eggshells, and our lives became a lot better. Whereas when Ed went I missed him desperately, partly because he was my baby and there were no children left at home, so it felt like the end of something. But it was also because he has always been a much easier person to be with – not necessarily better company, just easier to love.'

Acknowledging loss with optimism

The empty nest is above all an individual experience affected by family circumstances and personal history. So there are no rules about when parents are likely to feel worst, or how long sadness persists. But there is a general agreement among psychologists and psychotherapists that a crucial first step is to accept the significance of the transition. Rose vividly recalls how terrible she felt when her son, Jake, the eldest of her three children, went to work in Australia during his gap year:

'I needed to acknowledge the loss but with optimism. When Jake left I went into this huge grief: not for the young adult who was going, because he needed to go, but for the loss of the little boy who would cuddle up and had been breastfed. I had to face the fact that I have lost that intimacy: it's gone and it won't come back. But at the same time as mourning it I recognised that I didn't want it any more, because now the thought of all that intimacy with little children would drive me to distraction! It felt like a rite of passage that I needed to go through, to let go of that boy he had been and the mother I had been to that little boy.'

If intense sadness and tearfulness persists beyond the first week or so, and if it interferes with everyday life, it is important to seek professional help. Thankfully full-blown empty nest syndrome – debilitating grief and loss of purpose – is rare. But mothers can feel sad and hopeless at any stage of the empty nest. It often helps to view the loss as a form of bereavement that can be healed through a period of mourning; indeed, this is how the empty nest is often described by psychologists and psychotherapists. This is helpful because it not only acknowledges the significance and challenge of the transition but it also sets aside a period where you recognise the need to look after yourself as you move on.

Case Study: Clare

Before her nest emptied completely, Clare was already seeing a psychotherapist as part of a counselling course she was taking; she had also joined a therapeutic, 'visual medicine' painting group and started writing songs. She remembers,

'The psychotherapist said the children leaving was like a death, which really helped, because then I saw it as a proper grieving period I had to go through, a transitional phase of readjustment. It helped me to see that the empty nest is what it is; there isn't that much you can do about it. It's something you have to work through, and it will take time.

'Expressing myself through writing songs and painting, and working in a group, was also a great solace. Since childhood, painting has been a place and a space for me to express my feelings, and a way of healing. There is also something very powerful about coming together in a group and being able to express yourself, and the way people deeply listen to you and give you space; no one interrupts. It is a very different experience from talking to a friend.'

Although she is a therapist herself, Judith Lask believes that the majority of parents have the resources to get through the empty nest without seeking professional help and she emphasises the importance of supportive friends. She says, 'It is important not to pathologise these sad feelings. Sometimes it is as if people can't be sad or melancholy without the assumption that it must mean they need help. But really these feelings are just part of the human condition and the processes people go through. You get a lot of comfort just talking to friends and sharing experiences. Talking to a therapist can be very helpful if there are particular issues you want to talk through, or if your usual sources of support aren't that good; for example, if your best friend's daughter comes home every weekend whereas you never see yours, it can create a barrier. The idea of bereavement is also very helpful, unless it makes it into a more negative thing than it might be. Parents need to work through that sense of loss and remember that actually there are some very good things to come as well and that loss is only part of it.'

Parents find all sorts of ways of dealing with loss. The time-honoured way is to express complex emotions through painting, writing, poetry or music. Crafts are good too: even making quite simple things, rag-rugs and patchwork out of the kids' old clothes is a deeply satis-fying way of mulling over memories while creating some-thing for the future (as well as recycling). Jenni, a rug-maker and former Reiki practitioner, has a more unusual way of dealing with moments when she misses her daughter intensely: she sends her healing. I'm by no means suggesting this is for everyone, but Jenni's explana-tion of the way it helps her illustrates that just focusing your thoughts on your absent child for a few moments can make you feel better. It is a way of acknowledging, but not indulging, your feelings rather than pushing them to the back of your mind – which we have to do most of the time.

Jenni explains,

'Sending healing to Rhiannon makes me feel I'm doing something positive. She may not know I'm doing it, but I feel a connection and it makes me feel better. I could just as easily sit quietly and visualise her surrounded with light. I believe any healing can be helpful, because she is diabetic, and one thing that makes me miss her more is that I do worry about her health. In fact that's what made me explore Reiki in the first place. Of course, I'm aware that most people think it's crap, but some people say receiving healing can be quite strong.'

What to do with their bedroom

Once the child has moved out for good, parents have to decide what to do with their room. A bedroom has much more meaning than mere physical space. Some parents leave the bedroom untouched because they can't bear to close a chapter: packing their child's stuff away is a final recognition that they won't be coming back. Other parents can't wait to put the child's room to another use: as soon as they've left for university a younger sibling has claimed the territory, or it's been let out to a lodger. But unless it really is a practical and economic necessity it is advisable not to be too hasty. Ruth Caleb, university counsellor, says, 'The room is hugely important symbolically so, if possible, parents should make as few changes as possible. It may seem unreasonable to have the luxury of keeping the room just for that person to come back to in the holidays, but the room is symbolic of their right to be in that home. To use it for some other purpose denies that. Of course, kids are likely to agree to it because otherwise it appears unreasonable. But even when students have finished university the same is true: parents ideally need to wait until the child is ready to move on.'

Even adult children like things at home to stay just as they are. To their parents this hardly seems reasonable – after all, they are the one who has left – but the fact that they are going through such dramatic changes is surely why an enduring haven at home means so much. Rebecca, 25 and now well established in her own shared house, still feels a deep attachment to home.

'Just knowing that home is there, and that mum and dad are there, is the most important thing. If mum had told me she was going to turn my room into a gym or something I would have felt really rejected. I had a few school friends whose parents moved house as soon as they went to university. I can't imagine how that would be. I don't think

they knew how to feel because that whole time is so exciting
but traumatic as well: you're leaving this school you've been
at for all these years and this house you grew up in and
suddenly it all changes. I think some of my friends felt really
displaced. I think it's comforting to know that home is there
when you need it.'

Clearing out a child's room is a melancholy task, and it's
obviously less miserable if you can persuade them to do it
themselves or at least help. Jenni's daughter Rhiannon is
now 25 and established in her new profession. Every time
she comes home she takes another bag of stuff to the charity
shop; most of the time her room is used as a studio-cum-
spare room. This slow and incremental process of disman-
tling Rhiannon's home base has been less painful for both
mother and daughter.

It is understandable if parents want a more clear-cut
closing of a chapter; it's a sign that they can move on themselves. Two of Emma's three daughters have moved out, but
six months on the rooms are still the same. But because
Emma has bitter memories of her own mother's ruthless
clearing of her room when she was a teenager, she is doing
her best to be sensitive:

'I want them to clear out their stuff because I need to
acknowledge the fact that they have moved out for good. I
also feel they can't have a foot in both camps – although
of course they are always welcome to stay in their old rooms.
At the moment they are a chaotic mess; they look as if they
still belong to them. I keep sending what I hope are tactful
emails asking, "What are your plans for your room?" But I
still remember being furious when I was their age and my
mother cleared out my cupboards and threw away whole
boxes of personal stuff – diaries and scrapbooks – that I'd
kept since I was a child. I wouldn't want to do that, so I
just have to keep nagging them.'

Many families believe that what matters more than a room of their own is making sure children know they are always welcome and that there will always be a place for them in the family. This fundamental sense of security is surely as much to do with the relationship between parent and child as it is with physical space. Rose and her partner are keen to move on themselves when their three children have left, and she believes this does not have to impinge on their sense of security. She says,

'I would like all three children to feel they can always come back and share the space we've got – but I think that can be quite flexible. It feels liberating that we no longer have to have a bedroom for each of them and, because we rent our house, our future here is uncertain. Ultimately, we're thinking of buying a flat near some woodland, something that would have been totally impractical with three young kids. When they come to stay they could kip in the living room – or Nick and I could move out of our room for them, as we have done before when their friends have stayed.'

TIPS
Ammunition for empty days

- Make a selection of photos that *don't* feature your children: of friends, holidays and occasions you've enjoyed without them. It's good to be reminded that it is perfectly possible to have a fabulous time without the kids.
- Ask your child to make a file of photos, or get a selection printed. Often their pictures get absorbed into Internet files and parents never get to see them.
- Find something else to nurture: plants and seeds are a good start, particularly since they don't involve long-term commitment. This is not the time to buy a dog.
- Even sad phases have good days. When you're feeling

more positive, store up ammunition for empty days by making lists, including:

- Things you want to do when the kids leave – from simple activities which can easily be picked up and put down, to new ways to spend an entire evening, and long-term dreams and ambitions.
- Friends to write to, ring, email or visit.
- Weekends away and longer holidays to familiar places as well as more adventurous possibilities.
- Pure fun – dancing, comedy clubs, pub quizzes, karaoke, dinner with friends – anything that makes you laugh and takes you out of yourself.

Chapter 4

Fathers

'In the follow up to *Eskimo Day* [Jack Rosenthal's play about the empty nest], entitled *Cold Enough for Snow*, Bevis, the father of our Cambridge lad, comes close to a nervous breakdown. The Empty Nest becomes a chasm. He begins talking to himself, forgetting his routines, laughing and crying inexplicably. He loses his sense of himself, when the focus of his nurturing years is no long there. It had all happened to Jack.'

Maureen Lipman's postcript in her late husband's
autobiography, *By Jack Rosenthal*

Why the need for a separate chapter on fathers? After all, men's experiences feature throughout this book alongside women's. But the fact that men are often deeply affected when their children leave home needs spelling out, because the empty nest is still automatically associated first and foremost with mothers.

There are good reasons for this. For a start, men tend not to talk about it – so it is assumed, usually wrongly, that they don't feel much when their kids leave. And it is undoubtedly true that the empty nest is a very different experience for most men, not least because they don't give birth. Ultimately, men don't have the same biological link with their kids and so, it is often argued, may have less emotional investment. And because they are less involved at home they don't face the same yawning lack of child-centred routine that many mothers do.

Yet fathers have always been central to family life, long before the dawn of the New Dad. There is no question that fathers can be just as besotted with their children as mothers, and that they are just as involved in their lives in a myriad different ways. The fact that many fathers still see themselves as protectors and providers rather than nurturers doesn't diminish their sense of loss or make the shift of identity any less disconcerting. But the bond between father and child is very different from the mother–child bond, so it is bound to feel different when it loosens.

The current generation of fathers, who are more involved with the fine grain of their children's lives than their dads, are likely to feel the empty nest even more profoundly. Of course, the empty nest affects each father differently, and its impact depends on individual circumstances. So it's not surprising that expert opinion differs widely about how much fathers are affected: some say men are only affected indirectly, through their wives, while others insist they are affected as much as women.

A private sadness

The classic image of an empty nest father is of a bloke joking with his mates about his relief at finally getting the kids off his hands. Yet, for most men, this kind of bravado couldn't be further from the truth. While it is undoubtedly true that many fathers play down their feelings about their children leaving – perhaps not even admitting to themselves how they feel – when given an opportunity to open up they often reveal a deep secret sadness. Terence, for example, is devoted to his only child, and he was heartbroken when she went to university four years ago. He remembers here what it felt like when she left for university,

'In the months before she left I blanked it out. I kept telling myself, "She's got to go at some point, you've got to be sensible about it." I thought I had got used to the idea until one night I'd had a couple of glasses of wine with some friends and this Lionel Richie song came on and I lost it. It suddenly hit me: *I've had her for 19 years and she's going, I'm losing my little girl*. The more I talked about it the worse I felt. I was sobbing my eyes out: I've never been so upset.'

Many men are much more reticent. Adrian, whose two daughters left home five years ago, says,

'I've always thought I was quite open in my emotional reactions but, nevertheless, like a lot of blokes I find it quite difficult to discuss these things; I think analysing your emotional state comes easier to women than men. My friends might say, "You must be missing the girls" or whatever, but it's very much on that level – whereas I suspect my wife has much deeper chats with her mates about it. Yet I crave for the girls to come home; I miss them terribly.'

Charles Lewis, Professor of Family and Developmental Psychology at Lancaster University, insists that there are good reasons for fathers to remain slightly detached and apparently unemotional, and that it's a mistake to make assumptions about the intensity of what they are going through. 'Not being open and articulate about an experience doesn't mean you don't have feelings about that experience,' he explains. 'I have spoken to men who express deep remorse. On the surface they may say it's great, we've got time to travel or lounge around, but that is only a veneer. There may be all sorts of constraints which prevent men from being emotionally expressive. Missing your children is not the sort of thing you talk about at work. There is a certain amount of pressure on men not to mention these things. And even within the family fathers have not got the space to be the person who breaks down and says, "This is a terrible change in our lives."'

'Letting go' energy

Men are inclined to be more pragmatic and dwell on the positive: they insist that the child leaving is the natural next step, and talk about how proud they feel to have brought up independent, emotionally healthy adults (and so they should be). Johnny, whose eldest daughter, Hannah, is at university on the other side of the country, is typical of many of the fathers I spoke to. He says,

> 'I think the empty nest is different for my wife, Chloe, because of the strong umbilical connection between her and Hannah; I'm able to stand slightly separate from that, and to look longer term. And also because of work: Chloe has given up her career for me to do my stuff. I am an eternal optimist; I look forward to the next stage. I've seen my older brother and sister go through their kids leaving and I think life goes on, it's going to be different and we will have to adapt. I do miss my daughter – there is a bit of life that has left the house – but I'm not wringing my hands. I'm not sad because she is doing something she loves.'

This calmer, more pragmatic attitude can be hugely helpful to offspring who are in the process of leaving home, particularly if they're finding it a bit of a struggle. John Hills, a family and systemic psychotherapist with extensive professional and personal experience of the empty nest, explains, 'Children need a kind of "letting go" energy that says there is more than home, there's a world out there to explore, and it's OK to take risks, to go on a gap year or take a job far from home. Men tend to be better at that. It complements the sense of home as a secure base out of which the child can explore, the energy that says we love you and we're thinking of you even if you're not here. That is also crucial to a child's sense of identity. What's needed is a balance between the two.'

This 'letting go' energy can come from mothers too; single parents need to balance both. I know of at least one relationship where the mother is the one who promotes adventures while her home-based husband is more cautious. Their daughter, Millie, says, 'My dad is much more nurturing, he likes to mother us a lot, so I think it was harder for him when we left. My mum is much more practical, she sees things as character-building.'

'Traditional' fathers

Many preconceptions about men and the empty nest – chiefly that fathers are relatively untouched by it – are questioned by research. Studies in the 1970s of the kind of fathers we now think of as 'traditional' found that they were more likely to suffer a loss in psychological well-being than mothers as a result of their children's departure. In her book *Women of a Certain Age* the American psychologist, Lillian Rubin, explains,

> Contrary to all we hear about women and their empty-nest problems, it may be fathers more often than mothers who are pained by the children's imminent or actual departure – fathers who want to hold back the clock, to keep the children in the home for just a little longer.

At the time, the explanation seemed to be that because mothers were closely involved with each transitional stage of growth and separation they were able to adjust gradually to the final parting. By contrast it came as more of a shock to fathers who, because they were at work all day,

were inevitably at one remove from this gradual process
of letting go.

This still holds true for many men who, like Rob, are
taken aback by the strength of the emotion they feel when
their children leave. In his case, unfortunate timing didn't
help: two weeks before his son, Dan, left for his gap year
in Ghana, Rob flew to India on a six-week work trip. It not
only meant he wasn't at home to see Dan off but also that
he didn't fully take on board the significance of his own
departure, which meant that he wouldn't see his son for
seven months. He was preoccupied by his own preparations
until he left for the airport himself.

'Suddenly I realised I wasn't going to see Dan for seven
months and I just burst into tears as I was leaving. I had
been charging around organising stuff for my work trip and,
although we'd had farewell dinners, it didn't really hit me
until the last minute. I remember all of a sudden thinking
that this wasn't the way I wanted to go. Dan burst into tears
too. I was very touched. It made me conscious that I was
going to miss him in the long term, because we had really
bonded in the months before he left, when he was at home
working to earn money for his trip. On the plane I had
another tearful session. That was the start of a long period
of strong dissatisfaction and restlessness for me.'

Research also found that, as well as being unprepared for
the strength of feeling, many traditional fathers felt huge
regret that they hadn't spent more time with their children,
that opportunities had passed. It appears that regret still
looms large for many men, even if they have been hands-on
parents. Mark, who separated from his partner when his
daughter was three and his son six months, always spent as
much time with them as possible; when they were growing
up the children divided their time equally between the two
households. His daughter, Catherine, now spends most of

her holidays at university and divides the rest of her time between Mark and her mother. He says,

> 'When she left, part of the sadness was that I felt I hadn't finished my job. It was almost like I had missed an opportunity. I've been taken by surprise at the speed of it all, and the suddenness with which she left; I think I got one email in the first term. I wasn't expecting to miss Catherine as much as I do. Her physical absence is a manifestation of a change in our relationship which had already happened. It's just that I hadn't really noticed. It's a symbol of the fact that she had already grown away and she's really not interested in what you're saying; she's more interested in her friends. Once I realised how much of a new life she has, I recognised what has gone, or what is no longer carrying on. I also realised that there were still things I felt I had to give, even though I'm not sure what they are. It's become clear that that chance has gone.'

Does closer involvement make parting harder?

The trend towards fathers taking more responsibility for their children's care is most evident in single fathers and men who work from home. The novelist J. G. Ballard (author of *Empire of the Sun* and *Crash*) had little doubt that his close involvement with his three children, whom he raised on his own after his wife's death when they were seven, five and four meant he missed them more intensely. Like the playwright Jack Rosenthal, who is referred to at the top of this chapter, Ballard's work allowed him to be with them most of the time; he said they did everything together. In his autobiography, *Miracles of Life*, he wrote, 'The years I spent as the parent of my young children were the richest and happiest I have ever known, and I am sure that my parents' lives were arid by contrast.'

It is inevitable that for such involved fathers the loss of the day-to-day caring role has particular significance, because the contrast is so stark when the children leave. The absence of routine, the loss of the nurturing role and the feeling of redundancy are all too familiar to women.

Case Study: Charlie

Charlie also brought up his two daughters on his own after his wife's death when the eldest was five. In order to spend as much time with them as possible, he worked as a child-minder and in early years education, which was even more unusual employment for men in the 1970s and 1980s than it is now. Charlie's life changed dramatically when his eldest daughter moved in with her boyfriend at 18 and the younger one went away to university two years later:

> 'When they left I lost direction. I know you mostly hear mothers saying this but I found it quite difficult to know what my role was. I was always very close to both daughters, even in the teenage years; they came to me because they didn't have a mum to go to. I knew all their gossip and what was happening with their friends and how they were getting on with their coursework and all that stuff. And I found all the caring stuff like doing the laundry and the cooking very reassuring.
>
> 'As a parent, from the minute they go to playgroup their relationships impact on you. When they moved out, all that suddenly went and I missed it. Suddenly I hadn't got anybody to talk to me about their friends and stuff. So there was an emptiness. It wasn't loneliness, because I had loads of friends, but something was missing. It was a gap. My career was going really well but I didn't have a focus. It was about not being needed. I had this gap and I had to think about me. It was a shock, because I didn't really know what my purpose was any more. I didn't really know what I wanted to do with my life for me.'

No role models

It can't help fathers that they have so few role models. Most men don't remember their own fathers being particularly affected or upset when they left home. So today's fathers have little to go on when dealing with their own feelings. Dick's experience is typical of the generation who grew up in the 1950s and 1960s: 'I'm sure my father felt sad but he had an incredibly satisfying work life, and that really kept him happy. My mother never worked, so when we left she didn't know what to do with herself and got quite depressed.'

Dick, a food writer, who has been the primary carer because he works from home while his wife, Emma, goes out to work full-time, is naturally keen not to follow in his mother's footsteps. The key difference is that although, like her, he is based at home, like his father he has a career that he loves. Even so, he is apprehensive about the dramatic change in routine when his third and youngest daughter moves to France in a few months.

'I imagine that when Ruth leaves it will be harder for me than Emma in many ways because the emptiness of the house will be something I live with all the time. And it will be hard not to have someone to look after, because it's so satisfying. I'll miss Ruth coming home from school and making her a snack and her telling me about her day – I've always seen that as an important part of my role. With kids, no day is exactly like another day. Without them, the days will be more uniform, more predictable. And the kitchen, where the family hangs out, will seem like the emptiest room in the house.'

Relinquishing the fathering role

Whether they are traditional providers, full-time carers or a bit of both, the loss of the fathering role constitutes a dramatic shift in identity which can hit men hard – even if they don't always recognise what's going on. In some ways it is less straightforward and more disconcerting than it is for mothers, because while being a father is key to a man's identity, it is rarely central to his being in the way mothering is for mothers. Professor Lewis explains, 'The empty nest is more obviously an identity issue for women than it is for men, because parenting is so central to the way women construct their understanding of themselves, whereas men generally gain more understanding of themselves through their work. Studies of men who look after the kids full-time while their wives work found that they see it as "helping out" rather than their core identity. But, despite this, many men start worrying about their children leaving home years before it happens. I have spoken to fathers who say "I had my family and my little nest and I'm losing all the kudos and the identity that I had as a result."'

Midlife crisis or empty nest?

There are strong echoes with the parallel identity shift often described by mothers. Charlie, who became a single parent at 30 after his wife's death, had a pretty spectacular midlife crisis when his daughters left home:

'Being a dad is the best thing I ever did. Seeing my daughter born changed my life. When they handed me this little being who I was responsible for, who I knew I had to keep alive, I knew who I was then. I didn't before she was born. Her birth was why I got a job and sorted my life out. And when my daughters left home it was the opposite side of that – your babies going. It was very significant.

'I went wild; I kind of had my second adolescence. I was only 25 when I became a dad so I felt like I had some unlived experiences to go through. There was an element of covering up the sadness I felt, but it was mostly just very self-indulgent compared to the other aspect of my life, which had not been self-indulgent at all. This was for me, completely: I went out clubbing as late as I wanted, I went on holidays to destinations I chose. I had never lived like that before, so it was very exciting. I could leave the office on Friday afternoon, get on a plane and be in Ibiza or the Canaries for a long weekend. People now saw me as a single man, not as a dad. It was wonderful, but it was also a little empty. It eased up when I met my partner, Robbie, who settled me down. I slowed down and went back to a domestic life of a very different kind, and I'm very happy with it.'

Even men who don't go through an obvious midlife crisis still face a period of questioning and reassessment that can be difficult and painful. Family therapist, John Hills, says: 'When children are on the threshold of leaving home, parents naturally ask themselves searching questions: have I made as much of my career and my life as I should have? Where are the rewards for me? These are not selfish questions; they are legitimate questions that everybody asks themselves. Many people in their forties and fifties hit terrible disappointment that the discrepancy between their dreams and the reality feels so huge. The crisis this creates is painful but vital, because it leads to reflection and re-examination. Through thinking and talking things through you can come up with something which may be less than the ideal you aspired to but more valuable.'

With one daughter at university and the other graduated, Tom, a mental health nurse, is acutely conscious of his shifting self. He says,

'The girls leaving home has made me think about who I am. I feel my life is being reassessed all the time. I do want my own life now, but I'm not sure what my own life is, because it is so intermingled with my daughters. Twenty years of focusing on their needs – that is my life. My life now isn't necessarily distinct from me as a parent. Yet my identity is shifting because other important things are starting to come into play, which haven't for years and years. Whether I'm coming back to the self that was there before I had kids, or whether that self has now become something else, I'm not sure – I think it probably has. I'm not the same person I was before I had children, although there is a continuation.'

The midlife crisis has been embedded in popular psychology since it was first identified in 1965 by the Canadian psychologist and psychoanalyst, Elliott Jaques, and remains the butt of jokes about middle-aged men buying motorbikes. But even now it is associated less with the kids leaving home than career, status and age – which is perhaps another indication that work is more central to men's identities than fatherhood. For all parents, it can be hard to disentangle what's making you feel bad, because the empty nest almost invariably coincides with big changes in other areas of life. Meanwhile, watching your children embark on adult life is bound to make you think of yourself at the same age: what you thought you would achieve then, what you have achieved now, and the limited time left.

Even fathers who have been closely involved with their children, like Mark, are reluctant to make the connection:

'My midlife crisis is about "Where have I got to and where am I going?" – which is perhaps more a male thing. I'm having a midlife crisis because I gave up my career and I'm wondering why. I'm 49 and not contributing to a pension scheme. The empty nest is not a factor in making me assess the future – my career and my health is. I've got a few close friends who are seriously ill, and that really brings it home.

'Having said that, the fact that Catherine is at university doing the same subject that I did has made me realise with

a high impact that we've gone through a complete genera-
tional cycle. I can very clearly remember almost every term
of my own university experience. That became the life I have
now, that is when I met the people I am close friends with
now. I know a generation is only half a lifetime, but the fact
that Catherine is now at that stage really did impact on me
in a way that her being at school and doing A levels never
did.'

Reinventing your work–life balance

Big changes in family life provide a natural pause which
allows fathers, like mothers, to take stock of their working
lives and reflect on what they want to do next – even if the
empty nest feels like less of an obvious punctuation mark
in men's daily routines. For Adrian, the empty nest, combined
with a major health scare, was a welcome opportunity to
change totally: 'This has given me a chance to do what I
always wanted, to be at home. I'm the typical househusband
now: I always have dinner on the table when my wife comes
home from work. She now has a full-on, full-time job after
years of being part-time while I do all the washing and
domestic stuff.'

But for other fathers it can be a wonderful liberation –
just as it is for mothers – to throw themselves wholeheartedly
into work, free of family commitments, with renewed energy.

Case Study: Patrick

Because Patrick's job involves a lot of travelling, the feeling
of liberation is particularly marked for him, a single parent
whose stepson and twin sons all left home at around the
same time four years ago:

'I feel very carefree now. I can be away for a month and
it's fine, and I can enjoy travelling without feeling any guilt
that I should be in touch with the family and know what's

going on. Travelling was quite an issue when the kids were younger and it was very difficult for my wife. So in that sense my life is very simple, very easy. It's nice to be able to do my job without having to worry about its effect on anybody else.

'When the boys first left, I plugged very much into work to fill the gap and I took on new responsibilities, which kept me very busy. But it wasn't a conscious decision to find something else to do because the kids had left home; it was more feeling that I had more time and an opportunity to focus on this new challenge. But it certainly meant that I didn't have a lot of time to think about the huge change in my life at home, because I was occupied brain-wise and time-wise. Four years on I am still working a lot, and now I'm not sure if I really want to be. I've even started thinking about what I am going to do after I retire, although it's not for another ten years.'

Age is clearly crucial when it comes to attitudes to work, and so is the stage men have reached in their careers – as well as how much they enjoy what they do. Men who confront the empty nest in their early forties are more likely to want to give their all to a career than fathers in their late fifties who might be feeling the relentlessness of the nine to five. Having said that, some younger empty nesters seem just as likely as men in their late fifties to be factoring retirement into their plans. Meanwhile, unemployment will also be a factor during periods of economic fragility and weakness. The prospect of facing the double whammy of redundancy at work as well as in the family can be disconcerting.

That is exactly what happened to Tom, a mental health nurse who took voluntary retirement at 55, the same year that his younger daughter went to university. Although Tom has continued to work freelance, it was still a huge adjustment after 30 years of combining a demanding job with sharing the upbringing of two daughters with his wife, Lynn.

'In the beginning there were days when I was thinking, *Oh God, this is not how it should be.* I missed the loss of role and the self-esteem and the feedback at work and there were periods at home of feeling that it's not the same any more without the girls and really missing the way it used to be. But the good thing about early retirement is that I have more time for the things that I have to start doing to fill the gap that the girls not being around has created. So I give more time to my allotment, I go out for cycle rides more and I can make more effort to see other adults.'

Marriage

The psychologist, Professor Cary Cooper, believes that men chiefly experience the empty nest indirectly, through a spouse or partner who wants their support to talk through their feelings about the future. Whether this is true or not, most of the fathers I interviewed felt that the biggest impact of their children leaving home was undoubtedly on their relationship with their partner. Rob, who was in his early forties when he hit the empty nest says,

'What the empty nest has highlighted most for me is my relationship with Shona – I don't know whether that's a male thing or just me personally. It's a transitional time on a personal level; the relationship has worked for years but now we're moving into a new life and I'm questioning our relationship. For me the kids leaving home has coincided with work picking up, so on a surface level I have many distractions. But it probably means I'm a bit self-absorbed, focused on work and trying to make that happen, and I'm probably not very sympathetic about what Shona is going through – she misses them much more than I do. And I'm in that mid-forties thing of feeling the loss of youth, and wondering, *Is this my life?* I still want to continue in that

slightly excessive party way, whereas Shona doesn't. For
me it's the last gasp – can I still do it?'

What was most encouraging was how responsible fathers
felt for making the relationship work and instigating positive
changes – a far cry from the stereotype of the middle-aged
man who leaves the mother of his kids for a younger model.
Relationship counsellors don't find this surprising. They
report a genuine shift in men to look at the more emotional
side of their relationship, to want to make sure it is still
intact. Yet many women, it appears, still cling to traditional
ideas about men. Certainly, the fathers I spoke to were intui-
tive about the challenges ahead, understood how things were
changing and were keen to negotiate new ways of being
together.

At the same time, men rely much more on their partners
for emotional support than vice versa. Fathers have little
option as long as the empty nest remains a taboo subject
for most men. But there are exceptions. Perhaps because he
was on his own, Charlie found it helpful to talk to colleagues
– mostly women, but some men – who were in the same
boat when his daughters left 15 years ago, and he still finds
solace in talking to other fathers.

'I've got one particular male friend and we often talk about
our children and what that means to us and what their
boyfriends are like – that is a big thing for dads. He is a
real typical man-type man, but his concern for his daughters
is as deep as mine, and he's as protective as I am. If his
daughters have difficulties, he's off in the car to bail them
out. Sometimes people say my deep concern is because
I'm gay but it's not, it's because I'm a dad.'

Until more men feel more comfortable opening up about
their feelings, the widely held misconception that the empty
nest is purely a women's domain will persist. Things are

changing, as paternity and parental leave become accepted as the norm and fathers get used to the idea that the milestones in their children's lives have a massive impact on their own. There is huge potential for increasing mutual support. As parents' roles continue to blur, at least around the edges, men and women could learn a lot from each other's different experiences and come up with new ways of supporting each other through the empty nest and beyond.

PART 2

Your Relationship With Your Child

Chapter 5

Letting Go With Love

'How selfhood begins with a walking away,
And love is proved in the letting go.'
    The final lines of 'Walking Away' by Cecil Day-Lewis,
        a poem dedicated to his first son, Sean

'Letting go is one of the hardest things that parents ever have to do,' says the family therapist, John Hills, 'because it is about separation, loss and uncertainty about how the person you love is managing and whether they are safe. Where can you place your feelings of worry for them, or your wish that they are coping all right in the world? Parents don't suddenly switch off, we don't stop caring.' The transition years between 18 and 20-something are one of the most difficult phases of parenting as well as one of the most important. When children first leave it is hard to imagine how they will cope without you when they're sad or ill or lonely, never mind how you will cope without them. And it requires nerves of steel to stand back and allow children to make their own mistakes. Parents tread a fine line between interference and support, and constantly have to judge when to step in and when to button their lips.

Handle the letting go sensitively, though, and in the future your adult children will come to see you because they want to, not out of a sense of duty. What goes on between parent and child during this key transition sets the tone of the relationship for the rest of your parallel lives. So, no pressure then!

There are new challenges for this generation of parents who want to stay close to our children and forge a different, more equal, relationship. So this chapter is about how the bond between parent and child develops on to a more adult footing as they go through the different stages of leaving, either through university, with one foot still in the family home, or as they take their first steps in the working world. The good news is that many parents find the relationship improves naturally with distance and increasing independence. But, at the same time, parents can do a huge amount to make the relationship even better, to promote a new closeness that will last for life.

Taking the long view

When kids first leave in their teens it may be hard to imagine how the future connection between you might be, and it's natural to assume that the emotional distance will simply increase exponentially as the years go by. But that is too pessimistic: what seems more common is that the relationship ebbs and flows, and often, after a couple of years outside the nest, and perhaps a period of pulling away quite dramatically, kids re-engage with their parents as they begin to see them as individuals with identities that go beyond the role of mum or dad. This is most noticeable when there has been conflict and stress, but it happens in calmer relationships too.

The family therapist, Judith Lask, advises parents to take a long view of how the relationship might be in five, or even ten, years' time: 'Of course, parents feel that their adult children will just move further away and fill their lives with other things and you will never be important again. That is rarely the case: usually there is much more of a re-establishment of the relationship. If you can keep your eye on the future you may make slightly different choices. You may not pressure your child to keep coming home and having contact – you might just make sure that you get together every so often. Parents have to trust that in a few years' time circumstances will change and they will get much more connected to you. It's not like a continuum, where they keep going as far away from home as possible – there are lots of comings and goings. People will find difficulty with the process of letting go and renegotiating a new relationship if all that they are focused on is the loss of all the lovely childhood years, without recognising that there are some very good things to come as well.'

Staying close while letting go

Parents today face a conundrum: we have to let go of our children to allow the relationship to become more equal. But the new closeness, even friendship, which we aspire to makes letting go even more painful, and we expect to remain involved in their lives. It may be wishful thinking, but nearly every parent I spoke to said they felt closer to their children than they were to their parents; no way would *they* have boomeranged back to live at home. Monica is typical: 'I think it's completely different for our generation, because I know Asha in a way my parents didn't know me. I couldn't wait to leave my parents and get out of suburbia and I didn't glance back. I occasionally went home, but it really felt like duty. I'm much closer to my daughter; we speak regularly and we know so much more about each other's lives.'

Yet, without a blueprint, parents are not sure how to go about achieving this new relationship. Our own parents expected and encouraged us to be independent when we left – it wasn't just the choice of the child. And when we were growing up a less liberal style of parenting often went with a family hierarchy that didn't countenance closeness and certainly not friendship.

Case Study: Rose

Rose, who was born in 1960, was the first person in her working-class family to go to university. She remembers,

> 'My dad always demanded respect as the head of the family, and he still does. There is more equality between me and my kids and no traditional hierarchy; it's more of a shared exploration. But within that there is also an expectation that we'll still be the parents, that our children's needs, even as young adults, come before our own, whereas my parents expected me to be fully adult at 18 and responsible for meeting my own needs. And I wanted to be left alone.
>
> 'But because of my own experience I've had no reference for the territory since my son and daughter turned 18; it has been quite strange to realise that they still want that connection and they still expect quite a lot of support. They need us to be involved and take care of them emotionally – and to a lesser degree physically and financially. But there's no map. I also think this new relationship with our kids comes with a huge responsibility. I have to be careful not to say something spiteful, because I can see that some things go right in – my kids don't have the same armoury as I did at their age, they can't brush it aside.'

Staying supportive for longer

The goalposts have shifted dramatically for this generation of young adults. In the 1960s and 1970s there was a pretty standard sequence of milestones and cultural rituals that we could rely on, even if we chose to reject them, of job/renting/university/marriage/mortgage/children. Now, young-adult life lacks those certainties. These days it's just as likely that our kids will travel, do a degree or work, be unemployed, go travelling again, train or take a master's and then move through a variety of different jobs. In the meantime, they may dip in and out of living at home.

All we can rely on is that it takes longer for adult children to reach financial and emotional independence and that there is less of a clean break with home than there was for us. A report from the Equality and Human Rights Commission in 2010 found that nearly a quarter of the over-50s and 9 per cent of the over-70s provide financial support for their children. But money is only part of it. What helps most is continuing parental involvement and emotional support, according to research from the Economic and Social Research Council.

'Large long-term studies have shown that making the transition from adolescence to adulthood is very difficult now,' says Cambridge University psychologist, Terri Apter. 'Young adults who have support from their families make the transition much more smoothly and successfully and are able to be more adventurous and expansive in what they achieve. If parents feel they should not be helping them, because they fear it will undermine their independence, then young people really are left alone and they have a much tougher time.'

Caring at a distance

Continuing to be supportive, while at the same time letting go, feels like a contradiction. Certainly, parents need to adopt a very different way of parenting than was appropriate when their children were younger. They have to learn to care at a distance, to stay involved without interfering. When they first leave it takes a leap of faith to believe your kids will manage the nitty-gritty of daily life without you, whether it's eating healthily or doing their washing or living considerately with other people. Who doesn't feel a twinge of anxiety that no one will notice if their child gets meningitis or becomes seriously depressed? Who doesn't dread the phone call from A & E in the middle of the night?

Parents are at a transition: you can still be the carer who will sort out their problems at a distance, but you don't always know what the problems are and you can't see them coming. Technology may have transformed how easily we can stay in touch, but it is hard to judge how your child really is from the tone of an email or a text in the way you can when you see them. And many children only contact their parents when things are not going well or when they want something, so you get a false sense of their lives. You think they're miserable, but in fact they were miserable when they were talking to you and the next day perhaps they feel better – the trouble is, you have no way of knowing that.

How to handle anxiety

Where children are concerned, out of sight never means out of mind. Parents still feel responsible but have little control and diminishing influence, and that can be an anxious-making combination. This is a period when kids naturally take risks as they work out who they are and who they want to be friends with away from the inhibiting gaze of their anxious parents. It can be a relief for parents to stand back and allow this process to happen at a distance. But if teenagers don't eat enough, or drink too much, are very shy or prone to depression, parents understandably feel nervous that things might slide when they are no longer on hand. Even one bad experience in the years before they leave home, such as being mugged or ending up in A & E with alcohol poisoning, can dent a parent's confidence.

Parents should trust their instincts, according to Jan Parker, a family therapist and mother of three teenagers: 'There are points at which intuitively you know your child is at a different stage. And that what was once concerning, and that you had to watch very carefully to ensure their safety and well-being, they are now ready to manage. The person you might then have to watch most carefully is yourself, to make sure that you are remembering that they can do it now.'

Confidence also builds naturally over time. To put it bluntly, the fewer bad things happen, the more your confidence increases. And if when bad stuff happens your child handles it reasonably well, your confidence increases even more. Rose, whose two older children have been on gap years to remote parts of the world, says, 'I don't mind my kids having scrapes, but I like to feel they've got the emotional resilience, a toolbag of resources to draw on, so that they can deal with problems without being deeply scarred and learn from them.' It is also reassuring to know that if things go wrong there is someone around to help and always comforting to have the mobile number of a friend they hang out with – as long as it is strictly a last resort for real emergencies.

Being supportive without interfering

The biggest mistake parents can make at this stage is to assume that your children don't want anything to do with you. It's understandable given that all we've got to go on is how we felt at the same age. And young adults can give misleading signals: they may seem totally preoccupied by their new lives and bored by news about home, and volunteer little information. They are often busy when you ring and forget to call back.

There are crumbs of comfort in knowing that most young adults happily admit that they ring home more when they are miserable and hardly at all when they're having a good time. Former student, Rebecca, 25, says,

'Parents shouldn't take it personally when their kids don't call back, because at university you're running around so much that you can only remember to do things which are right in front of your face; you don't even remember to call half your friends back. So if you get missed calls from your mum or dad it's another thing to do and to feel guilty about if you forget. And at university there are no reminders of your parents, so you are more likely to forget to ring them, not necessarily because you don't care or because you don't want to talk to them.

'Whenever my parents called me I would always feel really chuffed, partly because they didn't ring all the time, unlike some of my friends' parents who rang every single day and always knew what they were doing. When my parents called it meant a lot – it felt really good to feel that mum or dad had been thinking about me. And it really helped to know that they were always there at the other end of the phone and cared, especially when bad things happened.'

How to show support

There are all sorts of ways to show support – particularly important when your child is finding their feet or going through a difficult patch. Adult kids need to feel that family life is there when they want it, and they still need your interest, approval and encouragement – and not just when they get promoted, win a prize or get top marks. Cards, texts and letters, no matter how brief the message, let them know you're thinking about them, and the same goes for little presents, photographs and food parcels. When I was living in a grubby student house my mum alternately sent me chocolate cake and lavatory cleaner. I was always thrilled to get something from home even if the Toilet Duck made me think of her disapprovingly pursed lips.

It sounds obvious, but the important message to get across is that you are always there and that your kids can rely on home as a source of security where they can be themselves. Life in halls of residence or shared student houses can be fun, but sometimes it can all become a bit of an effort. At times students crave TLC, their own bed and home comforts – and long to just be themselves. History student Katie, 22, has recently moved into a new shared student house and says,

'The great thing about your family is that you can ignore people and they don't get offended; you don't feel you have to entertain them. I feel like I'm in my own space if they're around. Whereas when you don't know housemates very well there is sometimes an obligation to stay and talk to them when what you really want to do is go upstairs and be by yourself or go to bed. At this stage I don't feel I can be rude and ignore my housemates, and I find that quite difficult. It's just a whole different way of getting on with people. I think you have to learn to be a little bit selfish and sometimes just say, "No, I'm going to do my own thing." Which is a good thing to learn.'

If you find it hard to let go

The ideal is for parents to be interested and available, a reassuring presence in the background who doesn't interfere. This can be a tough call, especially for parents who are inclined to be anxious, and many parents worry about being too controlling and overprotective. By the same token it is hard to step back if kids are worried about leaving home. Heidi, 21, had great difficulty separating from her mother when she first went to university; she left later the same term and enrolled on another course closer to home the following year. She remembers, 'I felt terribly anxious about being without my mum; she and my dad were separating at the time, and I was very dependent on her. Looking back I think I may have got the two anxieties muddled. I can see that she was anxious about me leaving, and about giving up that role. And I think that added to my anxiety about the whole situation.'

But it is the parents who feel they still have a right to know the daily details of their children's lives who most concern university counsellor, Ruth Caleb, because in extreme cases it can hamper their children's progress. She says, 'Some parents still want the sort of contact they had when the child was still at home; they ask for progress reports and phone their child three or four times a day. If parents don't stop contacting the child, he or she can't free himself in order to have a student life. I understand that some parents fear losing their children, but they should be reassured that they will come back to them in an adult-to-adult relationship which might be far more wonderful than it's ever been. But children can't do that unless their parents have let them go first. Painful though it is to do this, you ultimately judge your success as a parent by how independent your child becomes.

'You have to trust that your child is sensible and will manage, and that if things get desperate they know you will comfort them. Help them to believe that they can cope as adults and be aware that they behave differently in different environments. They are often more capable than we think. Your messy, chaotic daughter is the same person other people see as an amazing and competent young woman. And for kids who have had difficulties with social groups at school, who may even have been bullied, going away to university can be a fresh start and a total eye-opener.'

With three grown-up children herself, Ruth Caleb understands how hard it can be to let go, particularly if – as so often happens – parents' lives have revolved around their families at the expense of their own interests. She advises all parents to think about their own identity and to find new stuff to do. Ideally this should start long before children leave, but it is never too late.

Case Study: Beth

Beth certainly finds it harder to keep a distance when she is less busy; her daughter, Daisy, is in her first year at university.

'I'm realising that letting go is a strategic part of being a parent; it is a very definite contribution you make as a mother. It takes a very concerted energy, a bit like trying to let babies sleep through the night. On the whole I find it easier to step back than Martin, because my own parents were quite stepped back with us. But if I'm a bit bored or lonely it's quite tempting to get involved with issues in Daisy's life, whereas actually she needs to process things herself. At the moment she still wants our help; it's still "Mum, I've had a terrible morning" – it feels too close. I think it is better for Daisy to find her own boundaries, even if it means getting burned slightly. It's better to discover yourself rather than to get spoon-fed and come out OK but not knowing who you are. When Daisy worked abroad in her gap year there were a few times when I felt I really needed to release her from my expectations; she needs to be allowed to make her own decisions, and I need to relate to her decisions in a completely different way. She needs to no longer take my response into account in the way she did as a child. But it's quite frightening, because what you've set up is now rolling and you keep wanting to tweak it.'

Crises

While children must be allowed to make their own mistakes, there may be times when parents need to step in. Making this judgement can be a tough call. If kids are seriously ill or have an accident, it's a straightforward decision. But if they have a soaring temperature, or are having trouble making friends, or run up a vast overdraft, it is hard to know what to do. Parents who were used to trusting their reactions when they saw their children every day now have little to go on. At a distance how do you judge from a monosyllabic or tearful phone conversation whether they are badly depressed or just having a bad few days, whether they are getting hooked on drink or are just going through a standard young adult rite of passage?

Parents have to ask themselves about whether their

concern stems from their own anxiety – perhaps prompted by a newspaper headline or those apocryphal horror stories parents love to tell – or a genuine response to their child's needs. Intuition may still be the best bet as long as it is tempered by the recognition that when children are away from home it is easy to lose a sense of perspective.

What to do if you're worried

If you are really worried about your child, and they are at university, contact the counselling service. (Personal tutors are legally not allowed to give any information about students to their parents.) The Data Protection Act prevents universities from contacting parents unless there is a serious problem, and if a student has seen the counselling service it is confidential. But whereas universities are no longer *in loco parentis*, they still have a duty of care to their students, and most take this very seriously. Most have excellent counselling services, and it's important that parents make sure that their child knows where to go for help. If there is any indication that your child has suicidal feelings or intends to seriously self-harm, call the university's security office. They will be able to check your child's well-being and find help quickly, day or night.

Alice, who is now 23 and recently graduated, went to her university counselling service in her second year, and again just before her finals.

'I went of my own accord; I know other people who have seen a counsellor, so I didn't feel there was any stigma. It helped to a certain degree and it was definitely better than going through it alone. I was also quite close to my personal tutor and I talked to her when I needed to; I think the university was very good at pastoral care. My heart was broken in my first year, and about nine months after that I was quite depressed, but I didn't really talk about it. I regret not communicating more with my parents, but I felt I couldn't explain the situation to people at home because it was complicated. Not talking about it made me more depressed. Then when I went to see the counsellor I did start talking about it and it got easier, so I wish I had done that earlier.'

If kids are far away, parents need extra-sensitive antennae to spot warning signs. If they live down the road, it's easier to pop in, but it still requires careful handling and oceans of tact. Elizabeth's son Oliver also got depressed after leaving school before taking his A levels and moving into a flat with friends. Although they had not parted on good terms and their relationship was still prickly, Elizabeth, a nurse, made any excuse to keep a motherly eye on him. She bailed him out several times, sometimes paying his rent and the occasional bill, although she worried that this might do more harm than good. She remembers,

'He was unemployed for a long time and spent hours on his own playing computer games and smoking. I was worried that he was getting quite depressed. I got a lot of flak from my friends who said I was being too soft and I should stop giving him money, but I couldn't see any other way. I just had to trust in everything I had put in over the past 18 years. In the end I got quite panicky about him, so I took out a bank loan and booked a skiing holiday for us. I absolutely hated the skiing, but he loved it. The physical activity did him so much good, and he stopped smoking while he was there. That week got him through; it was a turning point.'

How often should kids come home?

Parents may feel sad if their child comes home rarely, but they are more likely to worry if they come home too often. It may be a sign that they are unhappy or not settling, and parents feel torn about how best to help. The general view at most universities is that it is advisable for students not to go home for the first month or two. And while this makes perfect sense in theory, it is hard to stick to your guns if it's your child who is feeling homesick or unhappy. Kiran, 23, who graduated a year ago, remembers, 'I hated university for the first term. Although I met loads of friends and went out a lot I was just really homesick. Freshers' Week was awful: I met all the people I'm still friendly with now but they were behaving really differently. There was this false enthusiasm. My mum persuaded me to stay by promising that if I still hated it at Christmas I could leave. She said I shouldn't come home for about six weeks, although she did come and visit me. And then one day I suddenly realised I was having a good time, and I didn't miss home at all. So by the time I went home after about six weeks I was happy to go back, and when the Christmas holidays came, instead of rushing home I stayed at university for a bit because I was enjoying it so much.'

Kiran's experience backs up university counsellor Ruth Caleb's advice that if kids are miserable it is best if they try not to run home; it is probably more helpful to show support through visits and regular contact. Knowing that a parent will be visiting in a few weeks' time can take the edge off homesickness and keep you going. 'If parents make it too easy for the child to keep coming home – partly because they're missing their child too and they want their parenting role back – it can be quite destructive. But it is equally unhelpful to tell kids they've got to stick it out and never come home. Parents have to trust their child to bear the loneliness that is normal when people go into a completely new environment and don't know anybody. They should encourage their child to recognise that other people feel the same way, that it can take time to make friends and feel part of something.

'If you automatically think, *She's in tears I want her home with me,* you are saying to your child, "I don't trust you to handle things." Sometimes they just need to sound off. It doesn't mean that the best thing is for you to go and rescue them. It's allowing them to use you to let out their feelings but having confidence in them to get through these different struggles successfully. Of course, if there is huge distress, it's different – then it is essential to seek help. Do encourage your child to visit the university counselling service which will be happy to help and support them, whether they are just miserable or very distressed.'

TIPS
Keeping in touch

- Don't expect to speak on the phone every day, even if you know parents who talk to their kids all the time. Take your lead from your child: some children like short catch-up chats a couple of times a week whereas others prefer a long conversation every two or three weeks. Others communicate exclusively by text.

- If they are always busy and never call you back, don't be put off. Find out when is the best time to catch them and, if it suits, set up a regular weekly time to speak. Try to see it positively: if they don't have time to call, it almost certainly means they are having a good time; it doesn't mean they never think about you.

- If they do ring up out of the blue wanting a chat, stop what you're doing and listen. They are still learning from your example: if you take time out to talk, they will too.

- Ask if you can have the number of a friend for emergencies (and don't abuse the privilege!).

- If they only ring when they want something, be positive: see it as a good excuse to talk about other things too.

Money crises

The relationship between parent and child can only really be equal when they are financially separate, which may be years in the future. So parents need to think carefully about how this is managed. Money can be a subtle way of influencing decisions and exercising control; that's why it can be such a source of tension. Kids usually hate having to ask for cash, and parents are outraged when the budget gets blown on vodka and frocks. Young adults should be allowed to make their own decisions, whether it's about boyfriends or careers or how they spend their money. However, it is not unheard of for students to blow a term's loan in the first couple of weeks, and the influence of peers with more money can encourage overspending. In any case, even the most frugal person can be thrown by a massive utility bill. So a discreet enquiry about the bank balance won't do any harm. Children must always feel they can come to you if they need help without losing face. And parents have to tread a fine line between constructive support and indulgence. If young adults keep running out of cash, it obviously isn't a good idea to continually bail them out, even if you can afford it. Instead, it might be worth going through their budget together, working out where they could make savings, the bills they need to keep money back for, and exploring ways of supplementing their income.

Nurturing the changing relationship

In the long term, most parents get on better with their kids when they are living under different roofs. Kids go through a personal revolution as they venture into the world, but parents are evolving too. Anne, a single parent with a daughter at university and a son about to leave says,

'I feel I'm a much better parent now than I was when they were young. Then I was just so caught up with trying to keep everything on the road. It's the level of worry you operate on. As they get older you begin to realise that (a) you shouldn't be interfering; and (b) they're OK. I think when they were younger I was quite domineering in a way and unwittingly critical. Now I can step back and don't go in with the first thing I think of. Maybe I find it easier because I can respect the fact that they've got their own lives to lead. When they are young you tend to see children as your possession. They're not, they're going to leave you, you don't own them.

'I think my daughter has come to see me in quite a different way too; she seems to find me much less irritating and more useful now. She uses me as a sounding board in a way she never did before. Sometimes I have to be quite patient when she rings up with a problem she wants to talk through, because her problems seem to have very obvious answers.'

Even the most tempestuous relationships can improve. Distance allows parents and children to step back and see each other in a new light. Meanwhile, an equal relationship becomes a real possibility as soon as parents stop all that daily servicing. Yet, in the short term, conflict and irritability seem pretty standard even in otherwise harmonious relationships, as both sides adjust to a new way of getting on. Often it feels as if parent and child are pulling in opposite directions, as indeed they are. And when they come back under the same roof – in university holidays, for example – disagreements and tension seem inevitable, at least for the first few days. Jenni says, 'Rhiannon and I still spar when she comes back, because she feels I'm on her case and I feel she is being very demanding. I get so used to her not being there; you forget that children take up a lot of space, emotionally, physically, in every way. But after a few days we get it over with and it's fine. We're very close really.'

It is not just parents who have to make big adjustments. Children too need to change, to become more sensitive to their parents' feelings and needs. This often happens naturally when they're fending for themselves. They stop taking full fridges and square meals for granted and begin to appreciate how much their parents do for them. And because they've got space to develop as individuals, to keep their own hours and find their own way of doing things, that allows them to start thinking of their parents as individuals too. (More about children coming home during the holidays is in Chapter 6: Your Changing Family.)

What will we talk about?

One of the biggest changes is in the way parents and children communicate – not just what they talk about but how and when. At home people chat if they feel like it; they can ignore each other without causing offence. A lot of communication is wordless. When kids leave, it is harder to catch each other at a good moment for a proper chat: you ring when they're out clubbing or in a lecture; they ring you at bedtime (yours, not theirs). It is easy to feel that you are getting the dregs, when they are hungover or want distraction from an essay.

At home, conversations kick off with casual enquiries about 'What's for supper?' or 'How's the work going?' Without such mundane starting points a big hole opens up which can leave parents struggling to make a connection. Within days you are no longer familiar with each other's minor ups and downs; kids can't see the point of telling their parents what they're doing because to them it's just ordinary. Parents complain about having to ask endless questions to keep the conversation going, and feel frustrated by the lack of personal information.

Some parents find a difference between sons and daughters; others put it down to temperament. Philippa, who has two sons and a daughter, is in the former camp:

'When I am with my daughter I feel that the contents of our minds overlap, so when she starts talking about something it very quickly resonates with me. There are never awkward silences or any need to search around for things to talk about. Whereas with both my sons it feels like the contents of their minds are completely different. I have to make an effort to connect conversationally, although not emotionally. In some ways the emotional connection is more intense and difficult to deal with because you don't know what's going on with them. You feel this incredible protectiveness and love and anxiety for their well-being but you have no idea what's going on in their heads.'

Visiting your kids

Visiting your child in their new place can be disconcerting, because it brings home how much things are changing between you. At home, parents and kids rub together side by side, but visits inject a new formality which, once the initial euphoria wears off, can make parents long for the way things were. The idea that from now on you may have to make an arrangement to see your child is a total change of tack after years of hovering in the background in case teenagers felt like a chat. If kids are flat-sharing it can be awkward to stay for more than a quick cuppa; however friendly their flatmates are, you can feel horribly conscious of being the older generation. If they are at university there is nowhere to just hang out together, so you have to meet in public places – cafés, pubs, parks – or go on outings. It can all feel a bit artificial, a bit forced, with everyone feeling at a loss about what to do next.

On their child's territory, parents have to respect that they do things differently and resist the temptation to roll up the sleeves and don the Marigolds. Elizabeth, whose son moved into a flat at 19, has learned by her mistakes:

'Now, when I visit Oliver, I have to sit on my hands because I always want to move the dirty crockery from the living room. There's a tacit understanding that I am his guest. I would never drop round uninvited. Initially, I got it wrong – I would pick up socks and say, "Can I put this washing away?" and he'd shout at me, but four years on it's fine. Now I never comment on anything, because if I did he would get really pissed off. Although I admit that when he goes away and I feed his cats I do a bit of hoovering and washing, and he is very appreciative.'

The best thing about visiting is that it offers a proper (if brief) insight into your child's new life and friends. It takes you straight into your new adult relationship. Perhaps for the first time they can take the lead, because it's their patch; they know where to go and what to do. The worst thing about visiting is saying goodbye. It's not just that you've looked forward to seeing them and that it perhaps wasn't quite what you expected. There is something so painful and poignant about seeing your grown-up child walk away and back into a new life that has little to do with you. Parents need to allow themselves space to reflect and absorb their new sense of themselves in relation to their child.

TIPS
Visiting adult children

- Plan a date that coincides with a concert or exhibition you want to see anyway – either with or without them.
- Don't expect to spend every minute together.
- Never turn up unannounced.
- Keep visits short and sweet.
- Let them decide what to do and where to go.
- Don't tidy up or clean their room.

Chapter 6

Your Changing Family

'That's a nice big car you've got there,' Alice said.

'I know,' Katherine said. 'I don't know what Malcolm was thinking of. I suppose once you've had three children hanging round the house and all wanting lifts at the same time, you go on thinking in those terms even when two of them are gone.'

The Northern Clemency by Philip Hensher

When a child leaves home it is not just the parents who feel it; the absence has a huge impact on everyone in the family. The whole dynamic alters: relationships between parents and the remaining children change, as do those between siblings, both at home and away. 'The empty nest is a family experience, not just an individual experience. Because of the intensity of the small family unit, the loss of any member is absolutely vital,' says Charles Lewis, Professor of Family and Developmental Psychology at Lancaster University. Yet parents are often so focused on the departing child that they forget that the children still at home will be feeling it too. Although that is understandable, given the sheer effort and emotional energy it takes to help a child move out, it is important to recognise that you might not be the only ones experiencing upheaval.

Roles within the family change constantly: a middle child becomes the eldest; an equal balance between two adults and their two children suddenly becomes two against one; the youngest in a big family feels like an only child. A child who is used to being part of a noisy family faces two adults across the dinner table, and there are no allies at home to moan to about their parents. Meanwhile, if an older child is away during their younger sibling's crucial teenage years, they may end up feeling like strangers unless parents find ways of drawing them together.

Changing family dynamics can bring unexpected benefits too. Siblings left at home may get on better with each other and with their parents. It is now the younger kids' turn for their parents' full attention, which the eldest child inevitably enjoyed in their early years. One of the unexpected joys of the increasingly fluid empty nest is that as kids come and go there are more opportunities for parents to spend time on their own with individual children. Of course, it's great to have the whole family back together, but time with individuals is very precious.

How younger siblings feel

Some kids feel the absence of a much-loved sibling almost as intensely as their parents; I certainly did. By the time I was 11 my sister and two brothers had all left home and, after growing up as part of a big family, I had to adjust to being in effect an only child and making my own amusement. There was a mournful sense of tumbleweed blowing through the vacant rooms of our suddenly too-large house, and I think I felt the empty nest almost as acutely as my parents. I continued to miss my brothers and sister horribly until I left home myself, and I can remember counting down the hours and minutes until they came home for weekends.

Case Study: Katie
Katie, 22, a second-year history student, had a similar experience as a young teenager, when her older sister, Rachel,

moved to Canada. Even though her three siblings were still around, it had a devastating and lasting impact.

'I was deeply attached to Rachel; she was a bit like a mum to me, partly because she was 11 years older and partly because I wasn't that close to either of my parents at the time. I remember missing her desperately and yet not really understanding why. She had always been there and suddenly she was so far away. I have this lasting image of being at my grandmother's house one time when she rang and I wasn't able to talk to her because I was too sad. Of course, mum was really sad about Rachel going too; there's a particular song which makes her cry even now. She always wants to go over there and see her. I'm sure that affected me. Perhaps if mum hadn't been so upset maybe I wouldn't have seen it as such a big deal.

'After that, I became much closer to my mum; at that stage my brother and sister were a bit too close in age to be close to. Rachel came back a few years later and stayed for about 18 months, but by that point I had changed, I'd grown up quite a bit and she had a partner. So she was not the person I had known before and we weren't that close. It was definitely a different relationship. Even now I don't feel I know her that well and that's quite sad. I've always found it hard that I'm not part of her life; it's hard to be part of someone's life when they're so far away. She was the one I was closest to, and now she is the one I am least close to.'

The novelty of becoming an only child

Yet, many younger siblings rather like being the last child left at home. The departure of an adult child often allows younger siblings to be themselves. Once the influence of an older, cooler role model is at one remove, younger kids no longer have to modify their behaviour by taking account of their approval or disdain. A temporary reprieve from competitiveness and the constant effort to keep up with someone who is always one step ahead can be a blessed relief.

And some children bask in their parents' full attention. It helps that, generally speaking, parents today are more tolerant of what the younger generation gets up to; they may also want to make the most of their time with the youngest before the nest empties for good.

Case Study: Ruth, Alice and Rebecca

Ruth, 18, is five years younger than her next sister, and while she jokes about her new role as 'chief daughter' she clearly loves it. She says,

'Before my sisters left I thought it would be tough, but I sort of knew I'd like it as well. I miss my sisters, but I love being the only one left because I get three times the attention: I love just being with mum and dad and hanging out. We do nice things together. If mum's not at work and I'm not at school we go out for sushi – my sisters interpret that as me being spoilt, but actually it's just because we spend a lot of time together so we find more things to do. Over the last year mum, dad and I developed this fantastic routine, which I wish we'd started when Alice first left. Every evening when mum comes in from work we watch an episode of the West Wing together while I have dinner and they have a glass of wine. It sounds bizarre but it's the best thing ever – it's the hour I have every evening that's fun and relaxing before I disappear upstairs.

'But I have grown quite territorial about the house now, and about our new routine. When my sisters come home it starts OK and then we get sick of each other and bicker about stupid things, and I'm like Mum! I think it must be hard for the other two to slip back into the family cycle. I love my sisters very much but we always get on better when there's just two of us, or when we have a bit of time apart

– then we have such a nice time. I used to worry a lot more about being left out, but I think that's just the younger sibling thing. When all three of us are together I often feel like the younger sibling; there's that feeling that the older two would rather spend time together. So I do miss them, but now they're not at home all the time we've got a nice balance in how much time we spend together.'

Ruth's older sister, Alice, agrees:

'Ruth and I used to wind each other up a lot and fight like cat and dog. So when our eldest sister, Rebecca, went travelling it was hard not having her around; also because she and I are very close. But as soon as she left Ruth and I got a lot closer, and we stopped arguing, I think because before we were always fighting for Becca's attention. I hadn't really thought about that until she left. Then, of course, when Becca came back Ruth and I would start bickering again! But now I don't see how I could get on any better with my sisters.'

Research suggests that brothers and sisters often reconnect and value each other more as a natural consequence of getting older. It is not uncommon for siblings to share a flat when they leave home. As they gradually leave the nest, relationships seem to benefit from the distance that naturally opens up, both from each other and from their parents. Harriet Gross, Professor of Psychology at Lincoln University, explains why this might be: 'Once children have started leaving home they have more engagement with each other about what their lives are like, separate from their relationship with their parents. They are more in touch with each other on a different level. They're not constantly sharing the same environment, so they have something else to bring them together. And, of course, now they keep in touch quite separately through social networking sites and mobiles and texts, and it's very different than if it was being managed by parental interaction.'

Meanwhile, the sibling left at home often acts as a kind of switchboard for communication between scattered members of the family. Ruth keeps her two older sisters up to speed about what's going on at home, and at the same time filters information about her sisters through to their parents. When Alice was going through a tough patch, her parents had a fair idea of what was going on, largely through Ruth. No one quite knows how they'll all communicate when Ruth leaves.

The parents' point of view

Relationships between siblings are notoriously complex, and the way they get on inside the nest is likely to continue outside it. When they first leave, adult siblings may not want to see much of each other, no matter how much their parents want them to be close. In the end harmony is more likely if parents don't push it and accept that their children might not always get on. It undoubtedly helps if parents are fairly discreet about how much they miss the absent child, and are sensitive to the way their own sadness might make the other children feel. Martin admits, 'I wouldn't say I'm constantly wringing my hands saying that I really miss Daisy, although the two younger ones would say I am. They say, "Dad, stop going on about Daisy, you're comparing me with her again." So I probably am guilty of that.' But their criticism is lighthearted – and all the better for being outspoken! Martin is far from miserable about his daughter's departure; he generally sees it as a hugely positive move.

Parents who feel gloomy about a child leaving need to recognise that this could make their remaining children feel second best. Equally, when the prodigal returns they should think about how their unbridled joy makes the rest of the family feel. That is not to say that parents have to dampen their enthusiasm but, as Professor Gross says, 'Parents need to be conscious of the knock-on effect and to try to manage feeling sad about one child without those feelings impinging on the other children. But because sadness tends to be focused inwards, the capacity to think about its effect on others is often lost. So, unintentionally, you can make the person who is leaving home feel guilty, and the person who remains at home feel inadequate. Yet the same feelings of sadness may exist in that child.'

It may help to tell your child how you feel, while keeping demonstrations of excess emotion private – sob in the bedroom, not the kitchen. Explain that you will feel the same when it's their turn to leave home. It is equally important to allow them to express how they are feeling too, without trying to second-guess their emotions. They may miss their sibling; they may not, and the last thing you want is for them to feel guilty if they don't feel miserable too. Some kids relish the prospect of life without a domineering older sibling, and in any case kids are often preoccupied by their own personal dramas. Most children, like their parents, will feel a complex range of emotions which differ from one day to the next. Everyone needs time and tolerance to adjust to the new status quo.

How parents are affected by having one less child at home

For the time being, family life continues in a way that will only come to an end when all the kids go. Even so, managing a smaller family requires huge adjustments, and many parents are surprised at how different it feels, both practically and emotionally; for example, parents who happily left a couple of teenagers for a weekend or an evening might not feel so comfortable about leaving one child home alone and may need to re-think how to carve out time for themselves.

Case Study: Anne

Anne, a single parent with a daughter, Jess, at university and a son, Adam, in the sixth form, says,

> 'This is almost like the reverse of the jump when they are first born from having one child to two, which for some reason is much more than double. I find it a massive difference having only one child at home. I miss Jess, and I miss that part of family life. I talk to Adam about it a lot. He missed her too, but it was such a growing time for him and he was developing his own interests. We live such different lives with just the two of us in the house. Simple things have changed: when she left we ate different food, stuff she didn't like. We still tend to sit down for dinner at the table, just the two of us, and the other day it suddenly occurred to me that he might prefer to eat in front of the telly – we've never done that. Jess leaving has made Adam and me closer, but I have to be wary about that. Not least because I'm a burbler – I'm always talking about what shall we have for dinner – it's too much and he's let me know it is, so I try to keep it to myself a bit more or just go into another room. Adam doesn't want to talk about what show we might see next Christmas, even if I do!'

Having a child or children still at home helps to soften the blow of missing the one who has gone. Yet, many parents, particularly single parents, are wary of becoming dependent on the child left at home for company and solace. But it only becomes problematic if it stalls progress: the parent from finding new friends and a new direction; the child from forging an independent life. One practical way of diffusing the new intensity and injecting energy into family life is to take in a lodger, perhaps a student a bit older than your child. It's not for everyone, and it may not be practical, but it worked for Rona, who was still smarting from her divorce when her daughter went to university: 'I felt a very big hole when Nicola left. My son and I started to become extremely close and I felt that was wrong, somehow, and not fair on him. We were already very close and did lots of things together, and I've always been wary of being too clingy as a mother. So I organised a Canadian graduate student to rent a room. Luckily, she was exactly the right person and she and Simon got on like a house on fire – it was really nice for all of us.'

Managing the changing dynamics

As the kids get older, age gaps between siblings matter less. Before you know it the baby of the family, who for years has been considered too childish by an older sibling, has caught up with them. When the kids are younger, parents instinctively adapt to these constantly shifting dynamics, but they may be less prepared for the process to continue beyond the nest, when the added dimension of distance changes relationships yet again. It helps that parents now have more time and emotional energy for the children who are still at home: this is particularly noticeable with middle ones, who in the past may not have had much one-to-one time with their parents. Martin's wife Beth explains,

'I was always conscious of balancing out how much attention I gave the girls, so I'm really enjoying the change in dynamics since our eldest, Daisy, went to university. She always got a huge amount of my attention whereas I felt that the second one got about a quarter of it and there was only a tiny bit left for the youngest. Having Daisy out of the house helps because when she is at home it's too easy to give in to her needs, because she's so articulate and very close to both of us. So in many ways it's lovely to have that freedom.

'Meanwhile the younger two rather like Daisy being away,

because she is quite highly strung and likes being the boss. They miss her very much but, at the same time, they're quite pleased she has decided to stay where she is and work in the summer vacation, because when she came home she completely took over the role of kingpin which she had before. At times they couldn't stand it, although all three girls are very close and they are always able to laugh about it.'

Balancing the needs of kids at home and away

Parents have to balance the needs of the children at home, which are in your face, with the needs of children who are away, which may be less obvious but will still need to be considered, and not just when a crisis arises. It is sod's law that demands from different directions invariably come at once: after weeks of plain sailing the absent eldest needs constant phone therapy for a broken heart while the youngest loses their mobile and the middle one wants help with a job application. And you can guarantee that when the absent child comes home for a visit, a younger sibling's dramas will soak up parental attention.

Family therapist, John Hills, is reassuring: 'It's important that parents think of the whole family group, because our attention tends to be drawn to the child making the loudest noise or who seems to be in the most distress, while the other children may have their own frustrated needs. It's a huge task of relational management, but that is what parents are skilful at. We can see the contradictions and complexity of a situation, whereas children tend to see it straight.

'You are managing individual egos and personalities who are very conscious of their relationship with one another. So it is vital to try to hold on to the principles of equality, although in reality there are some characteristics in children which you respond to more readily – that's not how it should be, but it is often how it is. And when you are living in a family you can't always see what's going on. A discerning parent will overcompensate in the same way that a skilful teacher knows how to encourage the bright children as well as the struggling ones. So, for example, if the child who is away says the child at home is being spoilt, you just have to listen and weigh up the truth of what you are being told and, if it seems fair, to acknowledge that, and if it seems unfair, to explain that the situation is more complex than it appears.'

Family gatherings

As siblings' lives become more disparate it takes more effort to get the family together, and it seems the only way to meet up is by making concrete plans. Suddenly gatherings that once happened effortlessly as part of family life have to be engineered, while family holidays take on a new significance. Formality and forward planning can feel alien to families who are used to a more easy-going approach, and it pays not to get too heavy about invitations to Sunday lunch. But parents may meet less resistance than they expect; surprisingly, adult kids are often the driving force behind celebrations and family gatherings.

Judy has three sons and a stepson in their thirties and forties, and a daughter mid-way through university:

'The kids are still my priority, and always will be, and I hope that they will continue to want to join in family gatherings even though some of them now have their own families and partners. We put the kids first because we want to see them. There are times when I consciously think I won't plan anything because although we love seeing friends, on balance I would rather have the kids around. Also in latter years I have become more conscious of wanting to weave memories around the home for my children, memories they still hook into, and that we have celebrations which centre on the family. I'm Jewish, and the home and festivals have always been incredibly important: the homes I have created throughout my life have always centred around food and the dining table. I think that has impacted hugely on what we call an empty nest. It feels more like a drop-in nest because everybody drops in a lot. But you can't suddenly achieve that – it is a way of being that is built up over years. It's important to me, and I think to all of us, that we have celebrations which centre on the family. I send the kids emails about birthday celebrations months in advance with the heading "Family Matters", and I mean it both ways. You could label me a control freak but they seem to like it.'

Family holidays

Taking family holidays with adult kids is another good way to get to know each other again, a precious opportunity to spend extended time together. After a few years of doing their own thing with their friends, adult kids often come back to the idea of the occasional family holiday. It can be seen as one sign that children have made the transition to adulthood and that your relationship with them has grown up. But don't bank on them coming, and don't be offended if they have other plans; there will always be another year, and anyway you can still have a good time without them. (For more about holidays without children see Chapter 11: The Other People in Your Life.)

Family holidays can be a logistical nightmare to organise and, like all holidays, they can get tense at times. It's just too tempting for parents and kids to slip comfortably back into their old patterns of behaviour and sibling rivalry. Speaking personally, I'm always taken aback to find myself reverting to mother-hen mode, checking everyone is safe and getting on OK, which is not relaxing for anyone. So while I would always much rather go on holiday with my kids than with anyone else, it brings back some of the anxiety of holidays when they were younger: have they got lost, are they drinking too much or swimming out too far? Thankfully, the feeling fades after a few days.

When kids come home for holidays

Family tensions are likely to be reignited when kids come home for short breaks or college vacations. Suddenly, it's as if they never left, but in fact things are very different and there are huge readjustments to be made by everyone in the family. For parents, the holidays can be an emotional roller-coaster. They have longed to have their kids back, but after the initial euphoria things may not be quite the way they expected them to be, and it can all feel like a bit of an anticlimax. You want to hear all about their new life, but they may be uncommunicative and just want to go out with their mates. Meanwhile, they may be confused by the switch back into their former life, suddenly conscious of how much they – and their old friends – have changed and are accommodating two different worlds, at home and away.

Ryan, 23, who graduated last year, has vivid memories of coming home for the holidays.

'For the first week or so I'd keep referring to it as "your house" or "your kitchen" and mum and dad had to remind me that it was my house too. Most of the time it was fine, but when I came back for long periods I found it quite hard, not because of my parents but because of my younger sister, who had become so used to ruling the roost. She was not impressed by me coming back and made me feel really guilty about being there. She obviously found it very difficult to readjust to life with me around, because if I wasn't there life would revolve around her.

'I assumed that my sister's feelings must be what my parents were feeling as well. So I felt I wasn't wanted and that I was in the way – that was really difficult. Whereas now I know it was just my sister being a bit of a tyrant. I talked to my dad about it and he said, "That's ridiculous, we love having you here."'

TIPS
Strategies for when the kids come home

The 3.00 a.m. anxiety

It's a mystery why, having slept soundly for all the weeks they're away, the gut-wrenching anxiety about whether your child is back safely kicks in the minute they come home. Understandably, they have got used to coming and going as they please, but if you explain your concerns you can come to some agreement that they will keep you posted about what time they'll be home and if they are staying out. It is also reasonable to expect your child to respect the rest of the family, and not make huge amounts of noise in the wee small hours. Having said that, earplugs are a wise investment.

Mess

Parents' most common gripe is mess: shoes and sweat-shirts everywhere, coffee cups littered about, sticky juice spilt on the kitchen floor, towels in damp heaps. Kids' most common gripe is that they can't find anything because their parents have tidied it away.

There are two options: constant nagging or lowering your standards for the few weeks they're home. If you keep tidying up after them they will never bother to do it themselves. But if you don't want to keep nagging and can't bear to leave the mess, at least resist tidying their bedroom.

Money

Every family handles this differently according to individual circumstances, but it is worth setting a few goalposts in advance about who pays for what and whether it is reasonable to expect students to make their loan last through the holidays. If they don't have a holiday job, the alternative is either to keep handing out the odd tenner or negotiate a weekly allowance. If they can, many parents pay fares to and from home.

Knowing that it won't be long before the next goodbye can add an extra pressure to get on well, not to argue, to spend as much time with each other as possible. If parents can relax, and carry on as normal, there will still be wonderful moments. University counsellor, Ruth Caleb, says, 'Sometimes people look forward to their children coming home too much and build it up and arrange things to do, but then the child has other plans, so the parents end up feeling hurt. When kids go home in the university holidays they are often treated as the kids they were when they left. And then the old arguments about never tidying your room or helping come back in spades. But actually they've changed, they've grown up, and parents need to take that on board. When they come back it's not the same: they're coming back partly as kids of the home and partly as visitors. There has to be an adjustment because the child is now used to being very independent, to coming in and going out when they want to, and so they don't necessarily handle well your requests to know what they're doing. To some extent parent and child have got to get to know each other again, because there is often a sense of: who is this person who has come back? Letting people have space is very important, not overwhelming them back into family life or bombarding them with questions.'

Some families describe an initial scratchy period before

relations get back on an even keel whereas others experience the opposite: a honeymoon period before everyone gets on each other's nerves. Adult children may dress totally differently and have newly strident opinions on anything from politics to ways of cooking pasta; it may be hard to relate to this new person who feels like a bit of a stranger. For the returning child it is confusing too. Beth says, 'Daisy came home in the last holiday saying, "Mum, I'm a different person there and when I come back I can't relate to home." It's easier for her to stay there, and not have to deal with that whole business of switching between two very different reference points, family and university friends.'

A degree of friction is par for the course, because university vacations are the time when the development of the new relationship between emerging adults and their parents is at its most intense. Hammering out a new way of getting on may be more stressful than parents imagined. It is also a poignant reminder that family life will never go back to the way it was. It helps to approach each homecoming with a fresh eye and avoid preconceptions. Time apart gives you an opportunity to look at your child in a new light – and vice versa – and not get stuck with old prejudices about their behaviour and personality. Family therapist, Judith Lask, says, 'Rather than assuming that you know how it will be, try to keep curious. We always tend to go to default situations in relationships: it's easiest to just get into that old pattern of what we're used to, partly because the feeling of going back to an earlier, lost stage can be comforting for both parties. The problem is that it may come with a lot of resentment, so it is much better to renegotiate and discover something a bit different. It's almost like saying: this is unknown territory for both of us, let's try to sort it out. It helps if you can talk about the new situation and observe some of the things that might be going on in it. There are always opportunities in change: each side might come to discover all sorts of interesting things about either their parent or their child.

'For example, the stubborn streak you were accustomed to seeing in your child might have developed into something really nice, like persistence, while hyperactivity might have been honed into a really strong focused energy. An element of trust is required, because there are things children can bring into your life rather than you having to pull the strings to get them to behave in a sensible way. The young person is discovering a bit more about their parents too, being a bit more interested in them and discovering new interests and things you can share.'

Both parents and kids need to make adjustments, but it is up to parents to take the lead. The aim is to create a situation at home which kids will be happy to come back to, without compromising your own new freedoms or skewing the hierarchy by letting them walk all over you. If parents are too strict, their kids will come home as rarely as possible (see Chapter 3: The Nest Empties Completely). What kids don't like about coming home are rules, conventional mealtimes and having their parents worrying about what they're up to. But there are plenty of things to like: TLC, a full fridge, home comforts, spending time with their mates, spending time with the family. So while tension is unavoidable, arguments and nagging can be minimised if you renegotiate some ground rules, and if both sides are prepared to compromise.

Saying goodbye at the end of the holiday, seeing everyone walk back into their new lives and readjusting yet again to the child's absence can feel like the equivalent of yet another violent mood swing for parents. Once they've gone there is often regret for not making the most of precious time together, or for arguments about matters that in retrospect seem trivial. Although it can be helpful to look back and learn, it is better to dwell on the good times, memories which will bolster you up in the months to come.

TIPS
When kids come home: cooking

- Be as flexible as you can about timings, so that meals are relaxed rather than fraught because you're waiting for them to turn up and cross if they don't appear.
- Don't expect them to stick to every mealtime, but equally don't rush to the cooker whenever they pitch up in the kitchen starving.
- Instead, make food which lends itself to leftovers, and which they can easily heat up themselves: stews, pot roasts, lasagne, chilli. Or buy nutritious fast food that they can turn into a meal quickly and easily: eggs, sausages, bacon, chicken pieces, pasta sauces. If they won't cook at all, stock up on nutritious snacks, good bread, cheese, salad and fruit, and make big jars of dressing – then they can help themselves.
- It's great if they cook, and even better if they help make family meals, but not so great if they use up all the ingredients for the evening meal at 3.00 in the afternoon or you come down in the morning to the kitchen chaos of their drunken fry-ups. Try not to fly into a rage if this happens, but wait for a calmer moment to explain why you were upset. (Having said that, exploding often works if you don't do it too often.)
- Be tactful about cooking tips, unless they ask, and don't throw your hands up in horror if they make basic mistakes. It is less annoying to be direct than make oblique comments like, 'Don't you heat the pan up first, darling?' On the whole I think it's better to leave the kitchen when they're cooking and let them get on with it, as long as they know the basics and that you are happy to help if asked.

Chapter 7

Your Adult Child

'I long to put the experience of fifty years at once into
your young lives, to give you at once the key of that
treasure chamber every gem of which has cost me tears
and struggles and prayers, but you must work for these
inward treasures yourselves.'
　Harriet Beecher Stowe, the American abolitionist, writing
　　　　　　　　　　　　　　　　　to her twin daughters in 1861

Before I had children myself I used to wonder how parents
could possibly have a grown-up relationship with someone
whose nappy they used to change. It still seems to me one
of the great mysteries of parenting: how the relationship
gradually morphs from one where the parent is in complete
control when children are babies, through one of authority
and guidance, and ultimately to something more equal.

By the time your child has graduated – or has lived away
from home for a few years – the relationship between you
has naturally moved on. The ideal of an adult-to-adult relationship is within reach, yet it is still underpinned by other
apparently conflicting elements, such as authority, guidance
and support. So it can still be a struggle to get things on an
equal footing, particularly now that it takes so much longer
for kids to become independent, whether they move back
in with their parents or not. Meanwhile, the relationship
tends to ebb and flow: sometimes you are closely involved

with each other's lives, sometimes less so. Yet the connection is always there. 'It is sometimes very difficult to see the invisible lines of love that exist in relationships. They are there under the surface, but at times they seem invisible because there is so much else going on,' says the family therapist, John Hills.

The relationship becomes equal

When your children are young, their grandparents' generation often tell you to make the most of these precious years and talk wistfully about the transience of childhood. But my wise father-in-law would have none of it: he always used to say that it was just as nice to have a son of 29 as a son of 9. At the time I smiled doubtfully, but now that my children are grown up I'm beginning to see what he meant. One thing no one tells you about the empty nest is the possibility it opens up of good relationships with adult kids: it's the upside of seeing them less and letting them go. While the less pleasant aspects of parenting – whether it's laundry or high anxiety – have been receding into the background, your kids have been maturing outside the nest.

It may take time, and the process of growing apart and coming back together can be painful, but the relationship changes enormously as adult children take their first steps in the adult world.

Case Study: Nina and Bella

After years of friction, Nina and her daughter Bella, 28, get on famously. Nina shared custody of her two daughters with their father after they split up when Bella was ten. Bella, who is the elder daughter, moved out of London, where both parents lived, at 18.

'My relationship with Bella has developed a lot since she first left. Before that she spent a lot of time at her dad's house, and when she first moved out part of me was quite relieved that she wasn't around, because she was pretty angry and rebellious. I worried about her going out all the time and about her eating – she had a slight eating problem – but didn't really know how to deal with it. I think I was in denial a bit as well as preoccupied by her younger sister who also had health problems. Her going away and then coming back to live here has improved our relationship hugely. We're now very close. Four years ago I couldn't have lived under the same roof as her, and if you had told me we would go backpacking together in South America last year I would have thought you were joking. Travel is a real make-or-break thing for any relationship, and in the jungle Bella did me proud: not only did she conquer her fear of spiders and water, and carry our backpack most of the way, but she was always cheerful. We're like good friends now, and temperamentally we are quite similar. I think it helps that there is no one else around – her younger sister has moved out and I've split up with my boyfriend, so there's no competition.'

Balancing care and authority

It helps if both the parents and kids are flexible and alert to the need to keep reinventing a relationship that is constantly evolving. Until this point, parents have continued to manage the balance between care and authority which has characterised the relationship from babyhood, but now moves on to another level. The family therapist, John Hills, says, 'Parental authority erodes as the children get older and there comes a time when you see that they can manage themselves and make their own sensible choices. It's at this stage that the relationship between parent and adult child can become more like a friendship, although it's a rather special kind of friendship, because there is still an element of authority. At no stage when they are younger does the relationship feel like friendship, and nor should it.

'The ideal as kids become adults is to create an open atmosphere between you so that both sides can learn from the other without feeling unduly criticised. It's about being open, and constantly checking out your own values and beliefs against your experience and where your children are. And it's about being prepared to learn from your children, and change some of your own views and prejudices and assumptions, as well as helping your children to examine their own. Yet this is a huge challenge for parents, because at the same time you're getting on with the rest of life, with the task of managing a job, a home, a relationship.'

Can parents and children be friends?

The notion of being friends with your kids is relatively new; in the past it was deemed neither possible nor desirable. Although many parents see elements of friendship in their relationship with their children, there are all sorts of reasons why it can never be quite the same as a conventional friendship. Children don't necessarily want to be friends with their parents either. Rebecca, 25, laughs when she says,

'I like my mum to be my mum. I like to be a bit scared of her! I definitely try to please her. So I'm always a bit suspicious of people who say their mum is like their best friend. Having said that, there isn't a massive boundary with my parents in the way there is with some of my friends, who see their parents as separate and removed. I really get on with my parents and I like talking to them about ideas and things I've read with them. I value their opinions. I probably speak to at least one parent every day, even if it's in an email or text. I see my parents as part of my constant life, just as much as my friends.'

Ironically, if parents try too hard to be on friendly terms with their kids it can increase tension. When parents are anxious for their child's friendship and commendation they find it much more difficult to assert their authority, so the hierarchy gets skewed, and it's not clear who is in charge. If either side is wary of upsetting the other, it hardly creates a sound basis for an equal relationship. If kids are at home, parents may feel nervous of questioning their behaviour, whether it's making too much noise or taking over the living room. If kids are away, it feels worrying to risk upsetting someone you might not speak to again for days. Either way it is confusing: if adult kids are now equals, can we still tell them off? Should we expect them to talk to us as they would to their mates (which rarely feels quite right), or should we expect an element of respect in the way they talk to us? Each family works through these dilemmas in their own way.

On the surface, Charlie appears to be the classic groovy parent who is best mates with his two daughters, both in their early thirties: they've been clubbing together, they meet at the same parties, like similar music. Yet Charlie, who brought the girls up after his wife died when they were five and four, and later came out as a gay man, remains very much the father figure:

> 'I still tell my daughters off: they don't like it, but I still do it and I feel I can speak my mind. If I'm concerned, I have to say something, even if I have to shout; I can't help myself. I also think they want it from me, and even though they may not do what I say, at least they have heard me. And they shout back. But we only argue rarely and we don't sit on grudges; arguments get patched up fairly easily. Without doubt it is a father–daughter relationship, and it is definitely more than a friendship; I wouldn't talk to my friends like I talk to them.
>
> 'I also love to bail my daughters out. I don't know if it's

a good thing, but if they are having difficulties I want to help. I think it helps me with empty nest syndrome too: I can't cook for them in the way I used to so maybe writing a cheque is fulfilling a need in me. It makes me feel that I'm still needed.'

When kids ask for advice

Given how much friction it can cause, it is surprising how often adult kids ask their parents for advice, and how often they then reject it. The force of their reaction, even when it comes to apparently trivial matters, often makes parents wonder why their opinion was sought in the first place. Advice is often a flashpoint, because it tests the delicate balance between authority, support and friendship. The relationship has moved on in ways which, for all sorts of understandable reasons, parents may be slow to grasp, and they are taken aback when their opinion either gets dismissed out of hand, is greeted with derision or precipitates a massive row.

Suzie's experience with her 27-year-old son, who is currently job-hunting, sounds all too familiar:

'My son often asks me to help with his CV or read the latest letter of application, which I am happy to do because it's tough out there and I have had 30 years' experience. And then he scoffs at my suggestions and we go into the battle zone and he says, "That's rubbish, I want to sort this out for myself." And I say, "Fine, but why did you ask me?" I want to give him advice but I also understand that when he gets it it's sometimes mixed with anger that he needs it. And I realise that by giving advice I'm not always helping him to feel he is doing things himself. It's the same old catch-22 and it can cause tension and rows.'

It is so easy for kids to see well-meaning advice as meddling and intrusive, or an attempt to control (and, of course, sometimes it is just that!). As always, it helps to think back to how what you said may have come across and try to see things from your child's point of view. Rebecca, 25, explains what it's like to be on the receiving end of parental wisdom:

'Now that I've moved out of home it's much easier to reject my parents' advice. While I was still living with them I would be so tormented if I didn't agree with what they said and if I decided to go against it I couldn't deal with it; I just felt really guilty. But there have been so many decisions that I have needed their guidance with; in fact I have probably needed my parents even more since I left school. The most recent was about work: I was offered a job at a company where I'd done work experience but the money wasn't good and I thought I had no choice but to turn it down. My parents told me to talk to the employer, and advised me what I should say. Obviously, knowing me so well, and having done things like that themselves, they could guide me; I just wouldn't have known what to do otherwise.'

Even if your child feels like a friend, your opinion carries more weight than a friend's advice would, not least because kids grow up wanting their parents' approval. 'As adults, your children seek your advice and input in a different way than when they were younger. And yet you are not just another adult,' says Cambridge University psychologist, Terri Apter. 'Parents do not shrink to normal human size: you remain a person who has this huge emotional impact on them. So there is a mixed message: I am grown up and can talk to you as if we were friends, but of course we are never just friends. There is this very powerful bond, and what a parent does or says will have a very powerful effect on a child, whether they are 25 or 30.'

Ultimately, it is up to the parent to take the lead in patching things up when either side gets upset, although sometimes kids surprise you by saying sorry first. Hopefully parents know by now that even if an adult child takes umbrage it doesn't have to be a total disaster. Part of a genuinely mature relationship is the mutual acceptance that parents sometimes get things wrong. Kids no longer see their parents as infallible, but nevertheless they still respect them. A solid, equal relationship between parent and child, like a good friendship, can withstand disagreements and uncomfortable advice; the secret lies in knowing when the relationship has reached a level where this is possible.

Dr Apter is reassuring: 'If you say the wrong thing it doesn't mean you are going to destroy the relationship. Parents need to realise we have to keep learning. You can negotiate the impact of something you've said after you have said it. It can even be quite helpful to see that your child is upset by something, because you can learn from that and talk to your child about it and explain what you meant.

'Young adults are not as touchy as teenagers. Also they are more articulate, so that if they complain about you saying the wrong thing you can use that as a point of exploration. They'll be better prepared to take your point of view if you say, "Give me a toolkit, what kind of response do you want? And if you can't answer now please think about it because I'm really doing my best."'

Learning the steps of a new dance

This acceptance of fallibility is intrinsic to the new way of connecting without echoing the patterns of childhood, which parent and adult child continue to develop. Although the relationship between parent and child matures naturally with time and distance, it may also need a bit of a push.

Case Study: Jackie, Andrew and Hollie

Jackie and her husband, Andrew, had a stormy relationship with their daughter, Hollie, throughout her teenage years. When she moved into her own flat at 19 the physical distance between parents and daughter automatically lessened the tension, but Hollie often reverted to her old ways when she came home. And so did her parents. Then Jackie – inspired by a television programme about animal 'whispering' – started to make a positive effort to be more assertive herself, and to stop colluding with her daughter's behaviour. She explains,

'Hollie is one of those people who goes into a strop if she doesn't get what she wants, which I've always found quite intimidating, because it's not my way at all. Even now when she comes home she'll often be in a moany mood. I used to respond by getting into that "poor darling" thing or just keeping out of her way. But recently I've found that if I start moaning myself – even being a bit stroppy – it completely changes the dynamic. It stops her because she doesn't get the same attention that she's obviously looking for, and a strategy that has worked for her in the past isn't working any more. I also make it clear that I expect her help with things like putting a meal on the table, simply by asking her in a very direct way. Our relationship is much better now.'

Andrew adds,

'Jackie and I decided that if we wanted to keep a window open for our long-term relationship with Hollie she had to be prepared to come home. And why would she want to come home if she is constantly attacked? So we took a new approach where we just tried to be there and not be critical and bite our tongues, and if we were going to explode wait until she wasn't around. That was a bonding period for

Jackie and me because we just had each other and we had to support each other. It was difficult because your children really know how to hurt you. They hold up mirrors to us – they reflect our aspirations and the sides of ourselves we would rather not look at. And while there is a rebuilding process going on, I still treat my relationship with my daughter with caution; it's a real fingers burned thing.'

How not to sound like your mother

In most families old habits die hard, and sometimes it is impossible to resist slipping back into well-worn patterns of behaviour. Before you know it you're sounding uncannily like your own mother: telling adult kids to remember their bike lights or to switch off their hair straighteners or asking whether they're warm enough. It's not surprising that our kids roll their eyes; they have, after all, been managing to do all these things without prompting for some time.

By the same token, parents often say that their kids revert to childhood behaviour when they come back under the family roof. Most of us are familiar with the phenomenon whereby middle-aged men act like schoolboys with their mothers, or siblings fall into the familiar hierarchies of their youth; we may even be guilty of it ourselves! Going back to our old ways can be alternately irritating and comforting. Andrew says,

'I will always bring out the child in Hollie, and she will always bring out the parent in us. It's always more obvious at home: when she walks through the door she'll be chatty at first but she soon collapses in front of the TV and reverts to being a bit of a teenager. I'm very pleased she still feels able to do that, but I wish she could be easier to be around. That's why I much prefer meeting Hollie outside the house: we have lunch and hang out and get on really well.'

Arranging to meet/visiting

Getting together outside the home often helps to put things on a new footing. It takes mothers out of the domestic context, and if kids are on their own patch they can take the lead in finding somewhere nice to go. Yet some parents – myself included – feel it's a bit sad and strange to have to make an arrangement to meet their kids, who afterwards go back to their new home. Hopefully we'll get used to it. Judy has no such reservations about taking her kids out for meals: for her it's one of the perks of embarking on a new career with a salary since her children left home. She makes a point of regularly meeting each of her five children individually, as well as organising gatherings at home for the whole family. She says,

'Even my sons, who are in their forties, still feel like my children; they respond to me as if I'm their mother. Yet it's now much more how I would deal with my friends: they text me and we make a plan to meet, and I love that. It feels like they are respecting my identity, that I have other things in my life. Whereas when they were at home it was just the opposite. There was this assumption that they would come home and I would be there and there would be food and I would be around to give them lifts to their friends'.

'Even now, when they come home, there is an element of them regressing to an earlier age and a sense of "warm security blanket"; they help cook but things get left around, the front hall is full of stuff and my youngest leaves her washing in a big pile. I enjoy the contrast and I can ignore the mess and slip back into that hippie bit quite easily. But out of the nest, like when we go away on holiday together, things are very different. We rent a big house about once a year for a long weekend for the family and we all feel we're grown-ups together. To a certain extent that is more like being with friends than when we are at home.'

Girlfriends and boyfriends

The arrival of a serious boyfriend or girlfriend on the scene has a radical impact on the way you get on – for better or for worse. A long-term partner can change the dynamics of the whole family and may bring parent and child closer: parents of otherwise reticent sons often find that girlfriends open up new kinds of conversation. It can also help put the relationship on a more adult footing. But equally it can drive a wedge between parent and child. An all-consuming romance is a classic way for teenagers to distance themselves, particularly effective if their parents don't approve. In young adulthood a serious long-term relationship is the first indication of a future in which your child will be part of their own new family and you will take on the dreaded mantle of mother- or father-in-law. If you don't approve of their choice, it can be hard to bite your lip, but parents need to be careful about offering an opinion. One wise mother says she always tries to focus on the good points and allows her daughter to be the first to bring up any negatives or problems. Only then does she give her own opinion or support her daughter's view.

Even if you totally approve of a boyfriend or girlfriend, it can be a shock to find that, perhaps for the first time, you are no longer the immediate port of call in a crisis, the first shoulder they cry on. Suddenly, your child sees the family in a fresh light, because an intimate outsider, however well disposed, can't help but raise questions about how you do things. New allegiances – jealous-making if they spend loads of time with the other family – can highlight your sense of loss and the feeling that you are growing apart. And that's even before they get married!

Caroline, who is divorced and close to both her children, has noticed a big change since her 29-year-old son started a long-term relationship.

'It's as if the last bit of the umbilical cord has been cut, and it's an interesting process. Now that his girlfriend is around, I don't see as much of Sean as I did, and I miss him. I know he's there and we still talk and they both come and stay. We're going through a period of transition where I'm not any less regarded or loved by him but his focus is his girlfriend. That's quite interesting – I have to keep slapping myself and saying he will always care about you. He said to me one day, "It's not a competition, Mum." What he's really saying is his love for me has not changed. But he has to go, he has to focus on the woman he loves, because otherwise it would be abnormal and I would worry about that. I think I had said something and realised as I said it that it sounded as if I was a bit jealous of his relationship. I probably am a bit jealous, because the relationship he has with his girlfriend is the sort of relationship I'd like with a man.'

Communication and privacy

Over time, parents get used to knowing fewer details of their children's daily lives. We can only hope our kids talk to us about stuff that really matters, while accepting that they keep some things back – and vice versa. Some adult kids are more communicative than others: many parents find they get more out of daughters than sons; however, communication doesn't have to be verbal. Indeed, that is what makes the empty nest so painful: it is your child's presence you miss, not just talking to them. Doing practical stuff together – whether it's fixing their bike or doing DIY in their new flat – continues the connection. Fathers, in particular, often express their emotion in relationships through doing things. Rob says,

'Trying to get any personal information out of our son is very difficult; it tends to be more factual. There is a severe male lack of communication, so the actual engagement is quite minimal. But he is always pleasant to be around; he and I bonded a lot over the past couple of years by doing things together like working in the garden and organising a local bonfire party. There's a strong connection between us.'

Meanwhile, if young adults are going through a difficult patch, parents may have to read between the lines because they tend to be more reticent and self-controlled than teenagers. Some parents can instinctively tell a lot just from their child's tone on the phone. For kids who are trying to establish a distance this may be irritating: I always bristled when my mum picked up on exactly how I was feeling, even when she was 200 miles away. Dr Apter explains, 'You gradually have to find a new way of engaging with your adult child which is age-appropriate. And this can be very difficult. Adult kids often don't want to talk about their unease in a job, because of pride, and they are able to control their anxiety and their needs better than they could as teenagers. Sometimes they would rather do without your help because they don't want your anxiety. For the same reason you may find that the daughter or son who talked to you about their romantic ups and downs as a teenager will no longer discuss a close relationship – or perhaps will wait until they've made a decision about it. So I think parents have to realise that they need to fine-tune their radar as to how things are going with their children. And they have to accept that some things are not necessarily going to get easier: parents are going to be very worried when their son or daughter is having a rough time, or being unfairly treated – all these things you continue to care about, and sometimes that is a surprise.'

Accepting your job is done

Ultimately, the hardest thing for parents may be accepting that their job is more or less done: you raise them to be who they are, and then it's scary. Allowing kids to sort out their own lives, and deal with the consequences of their mistakes, runs alongside the painful business of taking a back seat in their lives. If it coincides with new excitements in your own life it can be less painful. But sometimes parents feel they are only popular when they are useful, to bail kids out or to provide free holidays or unpaid babysitting. Parents are there to be taken for granted – but only up to a point.

Accepting that your child's life is separate is a slow process, and gives rise to a mixture of emotions along the way: sadness, regret, pride at their independence, and perhaps an element of relief that from now on it is up to them. Philippa's eldest son moved out of home and into a squat in his early twenties, and they used to spend a lot of time on the phone wrestling with his problems. Now that he is in his early thirties their relationship has moved on:

'My emotional investment in the decisions he makes has been withdrawn. For example, he's got this plan to go travelling for a year, and I really don't mind either way, whereas ten years ago I'd have been worrying about how that fitted in to his overall plan in life. Now I think it's his plan, not mine, completely. I don't have agendas with him: I'm no longer trying to push him in any particular direction.

'I think it's an inevitable part of him having grown up that the intense emotion has gone out of our relationship, which is a relief. There was a phase, which lasted several years, when he wanted to talk to me about quite personal things and I didn't necessarily want to to the same degree, and I felt a bit guilty that I didn't. Now our relationship is certainly different, and I think it has improved. We are still close, but he now sees himself as part of his own family unit, and it's like he doesn't belong to me any more; he is completely separate.'

TIPS
Giving advice

- Try not to give the impression that you know best. Make it clear that your advice is just one piece of the jigsaw and that ultimately it is up to them.
- Just listening and offering a sympathetic sounding board is often what kids need most.
- Try not to be too prescriptive; suggest ways of working through the problem rather than simply saying do this or that.
- Avoid offering opinions about a girlfriend or boyfriend, if you can. Let them bring the subject up first.
- Don't be too hurt if your advice is rejected.
- If what you advise causes an argument, remember that your opinion carries more weight than a friend's. Keep the discussion open by trying to find out what caused the upset.

Chapter 8

When Kids Move Back:
The Boomerang Generation

'Back when the children were still there Alison somehow
never envisaged a time when they would not be. Oh, she
knew it would come – but she never considered the
implications, tried out the idea of an emptied house,
listened for silence. They went gradually, of course, so
silence came gradually, and there were returns, and now
there is Paul again so the silence is tempered.'

Family Album by Penelope Lively

The boomerang phenomenon, which has gathered pace over
the past 15-odd years, has transformed the empty nest. Yet,
when the phrase first entered the national vocabulary it
seemed incredible, even a bit freakish, that adult kids would
want to move back into the family home. After all, in our
day it would have been regarded as wimpish and weird to
go home to mum and dad. But, as numbers have escalated
– about 22 per cent of male graduates and 15 per cent of
female graduates move back home, and the numbers are
expected to continue to rise – it has become perfectly acceptable among the young adult peer group. And many parents
secretly love the idea too. Indeed, it is only feasible because
parents have generally become more tolerant.

It almost seems as if we could be moving back to a more

extended family life whose members stay closely connected for longer. Certainly economics are already forcing many parents to question their assumptions about independence. The family therapist, Judith Lask, explains, 'There are many cultures where people don't leave the nest. In Western society we very often think people should be standing on their own two feet, but I think we have to be patient for a bit longer, because young people are in the process of having to sort out a lot of independence issues which in some cultures they don't really do until very much later in their lives.'

Yet the suspicion that it is unhealthy and infantilising for adult offspring to move back home persists. Paradoxically, our generation is partly to blame, because of our tendency to idealise the way we left home at 18. Parents reminisce nostalgically about how we left with barely a second glance, and were expected to stand on our own two feet, even if it meant living in squalor with a dodgy boiler on the wrong side of town. But that is not the only way, nor was it without its flaws. Perhaps, on reflection, we could have done with more support. In any case most of us left home not because we had more gumption, but to get away from the kind of restrictions we wouldn't dream of imposing on our own adult children: to have sex, basically.

The significant difference between then and now is that, financially, life is much tougher for this generation: huge numbers of adult kids can't find jobs, and unpaid work experience is often the only way to get a foot on the career ladder. Then there are the kids who do have jobs, but face years of paying off hefty student loans, and either can't afford to pay high rents or are saving to buy a place. Many people think this smacks of overindulgence, that our kids have been brought up to expect unreasonably luxurious standards and need to wake up to the real world.

It's not just about finances, though: economic necessity is entangled with a wider sense of insecurity. The family therapist, Kate Daniels, explains, 'Although the economic environment is a huge factor, there are other reasons why children keep leaving home and coming back, which are to do with emotional need. We are living in an age of uncertainty and perceived risk, where young people question where life is going. To keep returning home is also to keep checking out base camp; it's a source of security, a secure base.'

Another emotional rollercoaster

The increasing unpredictability of adult offsprings' comings and goings makes the boomerang experience an emotionally turbulent one for parents. Julia, whose younger son recently spent six months living at home, says,

> 'You feel very torn because although you love them and miss them you've got used to having a life of your own again without them. When children come back it's difficult because it upsets the dynamics: two's company, three's a crowd. It's not ideal for them either; I was always aware that our son would much prefer to be living a young man's life with his friends. He only stayed at home because he was doing casual work as he didn't know what he wanted to do.'

If parents are still in the process of adjusting to their kids' absence the new uncertainty represents yet another emotional rollercoaster. They may have geared themselves up for a totally empty nest when the youngest leaves, only to discover that an older sibling is coming home. Then they never quite know when their kids might leave again, how long they'll be gone, and whether they will eventually move back a second, third or fourth time. And just as they've got used to having them around they're off again. To complicate matters, it is increasingly common to have not one, but two or even more children living back at home, which, if nothing else, brings on a disconcerting sense of déjà vu.

Case Study: Janet and Susannah

Janet has experienced this kind of uncertainty to the max. Her daughter, Susannah, who is 30, has just left home after several periods moving in and out of the nest, including 15 months in South Africa with a boyfriend.

'There has been an elastic definition of home for Susannah; she comes back here between temporary arrangements and six-month lets. I love it when she's home – particularly since she cooks the tea! – but it brings back the way I felt before the children first left home. The months of anticipation were always worse for me than when they had actually gone: I felt very tearful at times, vulnerable and edgy. The period before she left for Cape Town was awful. It was clear that her boyfriend wanted her to stay out there and it was very open-ended; she didn't even buy a return ticket. So it seemed very likely that she might decide to live there for good. We didn't see her for 15 months until they came back for Christmas; he was due to go home to South Africa in February and we didn't know until a week before that she wasn't going back with him. In the end she didn't and the relationship finished. I was very, very relieved.'

Any parent with an adult child back at home rehearses the opposing arguments about infantilisation versus support every day: they want to help but worry that they are colluding in dependence and holding back maturity. In fact there is no perfect age to leave home; it's simply a question of what works for each individual family. In many cultures it is not considered problematic – quite the reverse – if kids are still living with their families in their twenties and even thirties. That is not to suggest that living with adult kids is easy, but it certainly doesn't help parents if they approach the arrangement assuming that there is something fundamentally wrong with a situation that they have little choice about.

Suzie, whose two sons, aged 27 and 23, moved back into

her London house after university, worries constantly that she is holding them back. Her younger son has a job and is saving up to buy a flat, while her older son is currently unemployed. She says,

'There's no doubt that being back at home infantilises kids. I'm still playing out the old maternal role of saying, "Why have you left your junk out in the hall?", "Tidy your bedroom": I find myself adopting a kind of naggy refrain. But at the same time they play to it: I think at some subconscious level they think, *Mum's still there to look after me and tidy up*, whereas if they were in their own places the process of growing up would happen faster. That's what I get angry and upset about, mess and cleaning. Last night I couldn't get through the front door because the whole of the front hall was a bicycle repair shop. I was tired and I got angry. Sometimes I feel that if they can't respect the environment they're living in now that they are technically grown-up I don't really want them here. I'm aware that if I were still to cook and shop and do their washing that would completely infantilise them, so we have a rule that we all do our own thing, and while it's a bit like a hotel, it's better because it encourages independence. Yet, on many levels, I enjoy having them here: being in effect a single parent I have always been quite close to them. We have good conversations and it's usually quite jokey: they wind me up and tell me I'm pretentious.'

Asking kids to leave

Most parents don't refuse their kids' requests to come home; however, there may come a time when they ask them to leave, which is never easy. Linda, who has a new partner, baulked at the prospect of being outnumbered by both her adult kids; fortunately her son, Colin, who had been back for a couple of years after university, was sensitive to her dilemma. Linda says,

'When Madeleine was due to come back too I thought it would be a bit funny having both of them living here at the same time, and that they would gang up on me! Colin brought the subject up: he said, "I suppose now Madeleine is coming home you want me to go?", and I explained why I thought it would be strange having them both back. It was fine because he really wanted to move out and the timing was right. But it was very sad when he cleared out his bedroom that last time and there were only bits and pieces left. I'm sure when Madeleine leaves I will be just as devastated. At the moment it just feels like she's on holiday from university.'

Most parents would baulk at directly asking a child to leave. It often works better to take a more pragmatic approach: to subtly ease them out of the nest rather than telling them outright that it's time to move on. Nikki says,

'My son moved his girlfriend in and they lived in our home for about nine months. It got to the point where we thought, *This just isn't right*. It was quite difficult sharing a house with a young couple who were trying to live their own life but under the same roof. They wanted their own place, but somehow they didn't get it together, although they were both working. We decided the best thing was to help them find a flat nearby, so in a sense we nudged our son out of the nest.'

Support versus tough love

In other contexts it is much harder for parents to suggest it might be time to leave, however much their friends criticise them for being overindulgent and bailing their kids out once too often. We've all heard of parents who chuck their kids out in sheer desperation because of drugs or alcohol, but most situations are less clear cut. In economically uncertain times it is particularly hard to tell whether young adults are making a serious effort to find a job, or just being too picky about the kind of work they will do. Cambridge University psychologist, Terri Apter, says, 'Sometimes you have to think, *Would tough love be the right thing now?* It is very context-dependent. While I think parents should be supportive and respond to glitches in their child's career path, I am not saying that if your children are living at home doing nothing you should accept that. I'm talking about young people who want to be contributors, whose biggest vulnerability may be their unwillingness to compromise. Parents also want them to find a job they really like, not something boring and beneath their talents. But we also want them to be realistic.'

Couples may disagree about how seriously their child is looking for work, and even whether it's wise to have them back at home at all. Fathers often feel kids would be better off cutting the apron strings completely. This makes life harder for the parent – usually the mother – who is trying to stop their child getting despondent and keep family life on an even keel, despite her own doubts about the situation.

The adult child's view

Often the person it's hardest for is the adult child, grappling not only with the feeling that life is passing them by but also a creeping sense of failure and dwindling self-confidence. Millie, 24, remembers,

'I felt I should have impressed my parents by coming back from university and excelling straight away. Although I got part-time work, I still felt I hadn't found a proper job, just bits of things. I felt a bit lost and I needed my own space to work out what I wanted to do. When you move back home you fit back into your parents' routine. So if I wanted to go for a drink after work and I came back while they were eating it made us all feel a bit uncomfortable – they'd want me to eat a proper dinner, not just grab something, but that would interrupt their routine. I appreciated that I was lucky to be at home, but I didn't want to be in the way and upset their routine.'

Blurring boundaries

The biggest challenge when kids live at home is the inevitable blurring of boundaries. When they are away, parents generally let them get on with feeding themselves, managing their own money and so on. But when they come home you are not only confronted by their mistakes, it is also hard to resist falling back into the old patterns of mutual dependence. So, while parents try to encourage independence by doing the minimum for their children, there are bound to be dilemmas; for example, if their mobile gets cut off, should you pay the bill? Should you include their posh shower gel and make-up remover in the weekly shop? If you're putting on a wash, do you throw in their clothes? If they ask for a lift, do you say no out of principle, even if you're free? At times, sticking to your boundaries feels like you're just being bloody-minded.

Relate counsellor, Denise Knowles, advises, 'When kids come back it is important to recognise that they have survived on their own and that you don't have to immediately slot back into being the parent. It's making sure you don't get seduced back into the role of mother or father and don't collude with your children who will quite happily slip back into the role of child. And recognise that you are now dealing with an adult child with capabilities, and you have to allow those capabilities to move on.'

If your child is going through a hard time, if they are depressed, or unemployed, or not in the right job, it is even harder to stick to boundaries.

Case Study: Suzie and Alex

Suzie, whose elder son Alex is depressed and lacking in confidence after being unemployed for a while, says,

'My official line is that money has to be earned, and that I won't just dole out cash, although I find keeping to that boundary terribly hard. I pay Alex for bits of gardening and other jobs around the house. I would never let either of the boys know that I would bail them out if things got desperate. Otherwise, if they are feeling a bit fed up they are never going to get work in a pub or whatever to pay off their debts. I think Alex needs to keep that edge of independence in order to grow up and make the transition. His younger brother, Ben, who has got a job, gives me £30 a month to cover bills, which is a symbolic gesture, but it's just so he has a sense of responsibility, to prepare him for the real world. I'm quite conscious that financial issues are imbalanced between them and that Ben might feel that I am always bailing out his brother, and that his brother is sponging off me. I think he is getting more irritated with him because his life is very organised while Alex's life is relatively disorganised.

'I'm aware that you've really got to check that your boundaries are consistent, but I'm not good at that when I'm exhausted and stressed at work. Sometimes it is really exhausting always trying to play the grown-up; you keep wanting them to play the grown-up. And sometimes you want to express your anger and frustration. I do sometimes, but I try to make sure that it's only when it is really deserved.'

Parents often find it hard to know how to help their kids get a job or find a new direction, and even harder to take a back seat. Rather than risk nagging by making direct suggestions, they leave adverts for courses or jobs lying around: a not exactly subtle hint. When my son goes for interviews we often end up arguing about what he's wearing, I polish his shoes at the last minute and then get in a state because he's going to be late. Even though I know that it's up to him and that putting my oar in is not just irritating but totally counterproductive, I can't stop myself. None of this would be an issue if he wasn't living at home, although I love having him back.

Tom's elder daughter has got a job working in a local school, but he is unconvinced it's what she really wants.

'Helping Cassie make the next move is the difficult thing now, and I don't quite know how to go about that, apart from managing my emotions about her being at home, and letting her make her own decisions. You feel you're nagging if you make suggestions: it's all right when they're 15 to say, "You need to get some interests", but you can't say that to a 22-year-old. She's her own person. And she says she's happy, but I'm not so sure how happy she really is. I have to allow her to do what she wants to do. She wants to move out, and I suppose that is part of the difficulty. Because, in a way, as a parent you are constantly being rejected, knowing that she doesn't want to be here. So while I like having her around I'm also desperate for her to be independent and happy.'

Some experts advise parents to treat returning kids like lodgers, by negotiating ground rules before they move back, charging rent and even drawing up a formal agreement. This may work as a guiding principle, but children will always have a different status to lodgers: they have more rights because they are welcome in every part of the house, yet at the same time are subject to higher expectations from their parents than a landlord could reasonably impose. However, it makes sense to define a clean break with the way things were when they were growing up by treating them, if not exactly like lodgers, as individuals who are mature enough to pull their own weight. Make it clear to the returning child, as well as to younger siblings, that they are coming back on different, adult terms

– that's what they'll want too. But this can only work if there is compromise and consideration on both sides.

TIPS
Start as you mean to go on

- Establish a new set of house rules through discussion and mutual agreement. Parents can no longer set the kind of limits they would to protect a younger child.
- Live as independently as possible. If you eat together regularly, kids should help with shopping, cooking and clearing up, or make a meal at least once a week.
- Respect each other's privacy.
- Don't do adult children's washing or ironing, and don't change their sheets for them.
- Don't automatically expect them home for meals, and don't cook for them, unless you have made a specific arrangement. Only then can you expect them to let you know if they've changed their mind or they're going to be late.
- Be consistent. If you expect thoughtfulness, you also have to be considerate. If you're going to be late, let them know.
- If a younger child complains about the older sibling's freedom, explain the change in status and that it comes with responsibilities. Returning children should consider the whole family's feelings and needs.
- Criticisms of the way you run the house are bound to make you, as parents, defensive, but don't automatically dismiss your adult child's suggestions. They might well come up with a better place to store the pan lids or a cheaper broadband deal.
- Give each other space by going away for the odd weekend and letting them know when you're going out for the evening.

Why parents like having adult kids back

The negative assumptions about the boomerang phenomenon are belied by the experiences of many families. The truth is that many parents enjoy having their kids back – I know I do, despite my son's complaints about slow broadband speeds and my irritation at his towels hanging over the banister. For me the disadvantages are minor: I couldn't care less about the house being the same as I left it in the morning, because as far as I'm concerned the odd bit of clutter denotes movement and life. Life without it feels a bit sad.

Case Study: Patrick

Patrick happily built a loft extension when his twin son plus baby, his stepson and the boys' girlfriends moved back while the other twin was still at home on his gap year. Since then there have been periods when the flat has been completely empty, followed by phases when each son has returned separately. Patrick, who is a single parent, says,

'I was very pleased and surprised that the boys wanted to come back. It makes the place more of a home, more domestic. It's been really nice having each of the boys here individually and with their partners at different times, as well as all together. My stepson and I had quite a difficult relationship when he was a teenager and it was really nice to be in a situation where we could be together and get to appreciate each other as adults. I think his girlfriend being around made it easier, more grown up. Because it wasn't just the two of us it made it a more social situation, and there was a different dynamic. It was no longer that you had to decide to either be doing things together or separately. It made it more relaxed, more casual – you'd walk in and join in a conversation, or not.

'The way I describe the time when they all came back sounds ridiculously idyllic now, but I don't think I'm idealising it. Paul's girlfriend talks about it as a very happy time, which makes me feel great. It just seemed like a nice family life. Looking back we could have got on each other's nerves in a big way, but I don't think I drove them too crazy, although I was aware that my housekeeping standards might be a bit lower than theirs! But overall it seemed a happy ship and everyone had their own lives: we were all out enough and fairly busy, so coming home and bumping into each other seemed like quite a nice social thing.'

By the time adult kids move back, younger siblings have usually left the nest, and their departure frees parents to focus more on older children, whether they have returned home or not. Until the nest empties completely parents can be so caught up with the needs of younger siblings still growing up at home that they may have taken their eye off the ball in developing a new relationship with older, absent kids. The empty nest is full of surprises, and one of the nicest is the opportunity to spend time with each individual adult child, and perhaps even live with them for a while.

One huge long-term advantage of adult kids and parents living together is that it allows you to get to know each other properly as adults; children get a more rounded picture of their parents and vice versa. In Suzie's view this is particularly important for mothers; it may even help build a new sense of self beyond motherhood:

'What I've found interesting about the boys staying at home for so long is that they see you in your working life too, they don't see you just as a mother any more. The boys can see my work is very important to me, and that while I'm still their mother, this is my life too. They see my work–life balance more clearly in a way they didn't when they were younger. Now they see me as me, in my professional life, and no longer engaged in the things that mothers with younger kids have to do. As a feminist, I think that's a good thing. I think kids who move out probably don't get quite such a rounded picture of who their parents are.

'But sometimes parents almost know too much; it is much better if you don't know the whole story. When Alex was working abroad, I was much more relaxed because I wasn't worrying about him. You're not having to confront his lifestyle and deal with it day in day out, and that does make a difference. The anxiety to do with personalities and histories can be as stressful as the mess. Inevitably, if you are physically close you empathise more with their disappointments and rejections. So, although I have faith in him, it would be much healthier for both of us if he wasn't living at home. In many ways it's easier with my younger son because he's got a job and he is planning to move out next year, so there is a framework and a sense of future. I don't worry about him at all now. To me that's a sign that he has made the transition, he's grown up and I have grown up too in my relationship with him.'

Their lifestyle in your face

This is the downside of continuing to live side by side: your child's problems and lifestyle are in your face – and vice versa. If they live elsewhere, you don't know if they spend their scarce funds on takeaways and new shoes or get drunk every night; when they move back you have an all too clear picture. The flipside is that your new life is in their face too, and as a result progress towards building a life beyond the family grinds to a halt when kids come home. New relationships and practical matters both get put on hold. Parents who are keen to make a fresh start by decorating and reorganising the house don't just wait because the kids might mess things up but because a lick of new paint is a symbolic statement of a change of direction. Couples who are rebuilding their relationship may get stuck; single parents may not want their kids to come face to face with new romances.

Suzie says,

'I have my own independent life, but I don't want to rub it in the boys' faces. My personal life became quite compli-cated after I split up with a long-term boyfriend, so it was more difficult for me when the boys came back. There was a period when I had several relationships and I had to keep a lot of it hidden. I had to make some sacrifices. I still feel that I don't want my kids to feel my current partner is more important than they are. That means that some-times they take over: they have first rights on the sitting room, for example. That is also to do with my feeling that I don't want the complexity of my life to be on top of them, I want to keep it a bit separate. That does make some decisions difficult. And it can be exhausting, because you are always negotiating between different emotional and social spaces.'

TIPS
How to avoid the most common disagreements

Money: should parents charge rent?

This is a dilemma if kids are unemployed or trying to save. Individual families have different incomes and priorities, but the general consensus is that kids who are working should make some financial contribution, even if it's just a gesture to help them realise that they can't afford to go out clubbing every night on £18,000 a year. It's up to you how much: some parents settle for a symbolic amount, while if they set up a standing order it makes payment relatively painless. Linda says,

'I didn't ask for any money at the beginning, because neither of my kids was paid much. After a couple of months I thought Colin should contribute something, and he paid me fairly grudgingly in cash. Madeleine was more pro-active and set up a standing order of £35 a week – not much but a contribution at least – it was her idea because she saw how Colin and I were always having battles whenever the rent was due.'

Money: what should parents pay for?

Again, this depends whether your child is employed and how much they earn. Either way it is helpful to establish guidelines early on, with the aim of encouraging independence. If your child is in paid employment, as well as contributing to their upkeep they should pay for personal necessities, like toiletries. If they drive your car they should pay for their own petrol and at least be aware of running costs. It is more difficult to stick to boundaries if your child is claiming benefits or dependent on you financially.

Mess

This is one of the things that upsets parents most: chaotic kitchens, grubby bathrooms, stuff everywhere. It's reasonable to expect kids to help tidy and clean the kitchen and other shared spaces, but if their bedroom is a tip, that's their choice. Resist the temptation to tidy it.

Kids often think they've done a good job of clearing up after parties when in fact the house is still a tip. If so, persuade them to have another go. Some parents still set rules about the size of gatherings when they go away.

Anxiety

Adult children should be free to come and go without telling you where they're going and what time they'll be back. But they are also old enough to consider your feelings. If you still wake up fretting that they're not home, explain your worries and come to some arrangement, such as texting if they're going to be late.

Territory

Kids don't think twice about taking over the living room and monopolising the remote control. They can be equally thoughtless about making a noise late at night. And for some reason – guilt, usually, as well as wanting them to feel welcome and happy – parents often allow them to get away with it. If parents don't assert themselves – within reason – resentment is likely to build. Even if you love having adult children back home, it is in no one's interests to make them comfortable at your expense.

PART 3

Making the Most of Freedom

Chapter 9

Taking Stock and Moving on

'Ben was her youngest, her last. When the others went, she had felt a pang, but there had always been Ben, there had always been the untidy, demanding, gratifying, living proof that she was doing what she was meant to do, that she was doing something no one else could do. And, if Ben wasn't there to confirm her proper perception of herself in that way, what was she going to do about the future? What was she going to do about herself?'

Second Honeymoon by Joanna Trollope

The empty nest is a significant crossroads that can bring exciting beginnings as well as sad endings; it is the dawn of the rest of your life. It offers an opportunity to pause and reflect on the chapter that is closing, to acknowledge loss and regrets but above all to celebrate achievements. But before parents can fully focus on the future and work out what to do with more freedom, they need to take stock. Rose sums it up: 'I wanted to acknowledge the past and the poignancy of my son leaving, but with optimism.'

The good news is that at this stage in their lives parents are well equipped to deal with a transition that feels devastating one day, exhilarating the next. Research also suggests that underlying changes which occur in the middle years – whether people have children or not – can increase a sense of control. Harriet Gross, Professor of Psychology at

Lincoln University, explains, 'Effectively, people become more skilled at coping, they become better at reflecting on how they might approach problems or get round them. Women in particular may feel more stable, more competent than they were earlier on in their lives. Research suggests that this coping is not affected by the menopause or the empty nest.'

That is just as well, because at times the coincidence of midlife events feels like a kind of evil conspiracy: the menopause, children leaving, parents needing more support, diagnoses of cancer everywhere, retirement somewhere on the horizon. Each event on its own would be challenging enough, but the combination can feel overwhelming. The perfect storm, indeed.

Facing your identity crisis

Many mothers, and increasing numbers of fathers, go through some form of identity crisis when their children leave. The whole basis on which your life has been founded, and how you construct yourself, has to be rethought. Whether women have full-on careers, work part-time or stay at home, their sense of themselves is so intricately bound up with the mothering role that it's not uncommon to feel lost when it changes so dramatically. Philippa works four days a week and loves her job, but still says:

'As a woman your sense of yourself as a mother is completely central to who you are. I think my husband's sense of himself as a father is very important to him, but it's not central. And I think the sense of protectiveness is much stronger for women too. When Ellie left, I remember feeling a physical gaping hole. Thankfully, it wore off quite quickly, which I was pleased about, because I remember thinking that I couldn't bear to go on feeling like that.'

This identity crisis is linked to the loss of practical, day-to-day nurturing, but it is also deeply rooted in the biological connection which goes right back to pregnancy. It can feel like the unravelling of the identity which women originally take on when they first become mothers. This involves a radical shift in the way they feel about themselves and the way they relate to the world, while getting used to the powerful new sense of being needed. Conversely, when their children leave, mothers have to retune their identity: they are still mothers but with no kids around to nurture, or to need them in quite the same way. Jan Parker of the Association for Family Therapy and Systemic Practice says, 'The empty nest can be as potent a change as other transitions which punctuate our lives, such as the birth of a baby. The impact of that change can reverberate not only through us as individual parents but throughout the family and beyond to our relationships with other people. With it comes so many shifts in our sense of who we are and how we are as women and men in the world.'

Like many parents, I find the loss of my core role discombobulating at times. Almost without realising it, my state of mind and my moods have for years been directly dictated by my children's behaviour, their problems, and whether they're happy at school and making friends. Now they are no longer with me the immediacy of that connection has gone, and it's left me feeling slightly adrift. Suddenly, my moods and emotions are my own – almost. As Terri Apter points out, the saying that you are only as happy as your least happy child is something you still say when your child is 40.

I know I'm not the only mother who, when children leave, wonders, *Who am I?* It makes no difference whether you have interesting work, because being a mother runs through everything you do in life. Chloe, a stay-at-home mum, says about her own experience,

'It's not that life's so difficult, it's just that I lose sight of
the point. You're not doing anything useful, so what's the
point of living? That is where the logic seems to go.
Everything seems slightly empty. You get into that whole
conveyor-belt thing of moving through life and decorating
rooms and plumping up the cushions, and it feels like it's
not enough but actually it almost is enough. I find that a
bit depressing – that's why I have to stand back a bit and
get a grip.'

What is required, explains Professor of Psychology, Harriet
Gross, is a radical adjustment to accommodate the new
status quo: 'Your children become embedded in who you
are. As those children move away you see yourself in relation to a slightly different version of yourself. Often we
judge our mood by how other people respond. If we don't
have our children with us, who either prompt a mood, or
reflect a mood, sometimes you have a sense of *Who am I?
What kind of emotion could this be? I'm not sure whether
I'm being positive or negative*, so that your identity feels
slightly ambiguous. You have to reposition yourself in relation to other people.'

The perfect storm

There are other factors, notably ageing and the menopause,
which contribute to this sense of shifting identity. Without
children you are suddenly part of an older generation. It
doesn't matter that you feel 27: the first time someone gets
up to offer you a seat is a wake-up call, a grim recognition of the way other people see you. When you start to
see your children embarking on careers and courses and
doing the kinds of things that you can remember doing
yourself not that long ago, you can't help wondering what
happened to the last 20-odd years. You have to acknowledge your mortality and your age, which you might have

been able to ignore while the parenting bit was still under your nose.

If your own parents need care or have recently died, it increases the feeling that you are moving up a generation. Meanwhile, if friends are diagnosed with serious illnesses – an all too common feature of midlife – it gives added pause for thought about your own life. It's a sad, sobering wake-up call. The menopause can also contribute to an identity crisis. Professor Gross says, 'Menopausal changes can leave women with uncertain and conflicting feelings of irritation, frustration and a free-floating kind of emotional instability. At the same time there is the sudden shift to questions about, "What kind of person am I? I'm no longer a fertile person; I'm no longer a young person." Your age is no longer measured by the age of your children, but solely by people's view of you. And, depending on your age, the empty nest often coincides with an impending loss of usefulness at work. This reflects back to a lost sense of identity.'

It seems a particularly cruel twist that mothers who are already worried about their children leaving home are often made more anxious, moody and miserable by the menopause. It may not always coincide, and some lucky women sail through with minor symptoms. But the likelihood is that the menopause and the empty nest will have a complementary effect. If so, it helps to feel an element of control over symptoms by looking into the wide range of remedies now available and finding the best combination. These days it no longer has to be an either/or choice between the conventional, HRT, route and complementary remedies, which include anything from acupuncture and daily supplements (usually containing phyto-oestrogens) to diet and exercise. The integrated approach advocated by some doctors, including the leading gynaecologist, Michael Dooley (see Resources), encourages women to feel more positive by taking more control.

Challenging negative images

Although real women's lives have moved on, the empty nest still conjures up an old-fashioned stereotype of a jaded middle-aged housewife with too much time on her hands. The reality is as different and as complicated as are the lives of mothers today, but the image is still very potent: many women referred to the kind of 'sad middle-aged women' they were determined not to become. Rose says indignantly: 'I'm not just some redundant menopausal woman who hasn't got anything better to do than grieve for my children leaving home. What you go through when your children leave is so poignant and powerful, yet it's dismissed as being a bit cheesy. Even women who are going through the same thing sometimes make me feel energetically as if I'm signing up for my old age pension.'

The high value placed on youth gives empty nesters good reason to feel gloomy about ageing. The sense of being dismissed and ignored is surely linked to the invisibility that middle-aged women often complain about. It's not just in their imagination. In 2009 a survey in the *Stage* magazine found that over 80 per cent of people felt that women over the age of 40 were not represented on stage or on screen. Thankfully there are signs that this may be changing.

Forging a new identity

Adopting a strong identity beyond motherhood can be a challenge. External circumstances and timing play a big part: it tends to be easier for women who have had time to develop an emotional investment in activities and people outside the family, for example.

Case Study: Judy

Judy, 64, came to a career, and with it a new identity outside the family, late in life. At 21 she left her parents' home to marry, and from the age of 22, when her first son was born, her identity was totally bound up with her five children, now aged between 20 and 41.

'When I left home my father handed my passport and all my other documents over to my first husband. And maybe this is one of the reasons why my identity eventually became so important to me. But it's really hard to think of yourself as a whole person when you're a mum of young children. So I created my identity through clothes and I still do to a certain extent: in the seventies I was an earth mother with flowing skirts.

'I don't feel lost without my children – I think that's because I had another identity to go to, because my work really took off when my youngest child was about 16 – otherwise it would suddenly have been a question of, "What now?" It wasn't intentional, it just happened at the right time. When we saw our youngest child off at the airport last year I was very aware of my role in life changing, and I felt ready for it.'

How to deal with regret

The empty nest is a time of grieving for things that haven't been, as well as the things you've lost: the past opportunities you can no longer take up both in your own life and with your child. Regret is a particular feature of the current generation of mothers, who were often forced to make tough choices about juggling work and children and can't help looking back and wondering, *What if?* When the domestic pace lets up, there is pause for thought and reconsideration.

Like a lot of mothers, I feel divided: one minute I wish I could reclaim all those weekends I spent working rather than taking my kids to the park, and the next I'm regretting career opportunities I turned down because of the family. Many women remember the huge pressure to try to have it all, and in retrospect wish they hadn't worked such long hours. Research suggests that for working mothers the empty nest is less about missing the daily routines of parenting than about looking back, often with some regret that the opportunity to do stuff with the children has passed. But stay-at-home mothers are just as likely to feel regret about activities they never got round to or for not enjoying their children enough.

In this respect attitudes have changed radically since the days when women had little option but to give up work to raise families. Research in the US in the 1970s by Dr Lillian Rubin found that stay-at-home mothers felt less regret than fathers, who never had enough time to spend with their children. This is surely because full-time mothers felt they had given parenting their full attention and weren't distracted by other demands on their attention. They had also had enough of being at home. In any case, they didn't have much choice. Mothers today, whether they work part-time, full-time or from home, feel less certain that the decisions they made were right. It's not much easier for women who choose to stay at home: now that expectations of 'fulfilment' are so high, they often look back wistfully at years of full-time parenting and feel they could have achieved more.

So how can parents deal with regret? Talking to younger parents can offer a useful reality check, which puts past decisions into perspective. The current struggles of families with young children are a reminder that decisions about parenting are never straightforward and compromises are tough. It may look like bliss through rose-tinted spectacles – all picnics and cosy bedtimes – but when you are actually going through it parenting is about rushing to get everyone to school on time, sorting out arguments and nit combs. If parents are honest, it is a huge relief to have got through the agonies about school places and childcare and managing when little ones were ill.

Stay-at-home mother, Chloe, says of her personal experience,

'I talk to a lot of young mums through my connection with our church and that makes me realise that all the anxiety I felt in the past about choices was really not so important; it's all relational. However, I still look back at those early stages with some anxiety – especially feeling that I didn't spend much time enjoying the children when they were little, but when I see the pressures that families are under, juggling all the responsibilities as well as just trying to keep relationships going well, it helps me see that I didn't make such bad choices after all, and maybe we did even have a normal amount of fun together. I find that talking to young parents affirms me. It makes me feel OK, that I did do some things right and it was a valuable time of life. That is really helpful. At the moment I am mentoring a woman who is about to move to a developing country, which is what I did when our children were younger. Talking to her about her life has been very helpful; it's a kind of debriefing for me. It pulls me out of myself and stops me feeling sorry for myself.'

Although you can never get a child's early years back, the empty nest offers parents a chance to build new relationships with adult children and to take up career opportunities they missed because of family responsibilities. In her late forties Julia, a lawyer, was given an opportunity to lay to rest an ambition she had nursed for years, of getting a position in a prestigious firm. She had always opted for part-time jobs that fitted around her four children. Then, in anticipation of the empty nest, when her youngest was 15, she was offered her dream job and jumped at it.

'I had always felt that certain doors were permanently closed to me, because I had only worked part-time and so hadn't built up the relevant experience. I had always wondered, *What if?* I didn't have the opportunity when I was younger, because I was the one responsible for the family and Mike worked away a lot. So while I could do a professional job I could not have done a more demanding one. But, as the empty nest approached, I felt there was an opportunity to prove to myself that I still had the ability and the drive. So this job was a chance for me to prove to myself that I had the ability, to scratch the itch I had always had. I was thrilled to get it, but it turned out to be a real eye-opener. It made me realise I hadn't missed out at all – no way would I have wanted to spend my whole professional life in a place like that.'

Celebrate your achievements

What should help parents manage regret and loss most is recognising their fantastic achievements as parents: just look at your fabulous offspring! Bringing up children who are healthy, independent and ready to leave is ultimately what parenting is all about. Men tend to be better at emphasising their pride in their kids than women, who are more inclined to dwell on doubts about mistakes, past and present.

So why don't women celebrate more? It's partly because the quiet job of parenting, despite all the guff about it in the media, is still so gravely undervalued. The family therapist John Hills says, 'Bringing up children requires a level of saintliness not recognised in our culture; it is the most altruistic task we are called on to do. To survive it and come through with your children healthy and independent is a hell of an accomplishment.' Yet, most of the time, bringing up kids feels like such a mundane accumulation of everyday routines and domestic crises that it's hard to feel you've done anything more than make packed lunches, sort socks and give people lifts for 20 years.

Some women I spoke to felt strongly that all those years of parenting needed marking or celebrating in some way which has nothing to do with graduation ceremonies or music prizes or football trophies. They came up with intriguing ways of doing this: some organised formal celebrations involving the extended family, whereas others were more private: they compiled photograph albums charting significant moments in the child's life (often as presents for the child), or made gifts, or wrote stories or songs, or letters to their children.

Case Study: Rose

The day her son flew to Australia, Rose immersed herself in old family photographs, and made a collage charting their life together from pregnancy onwards. She remembers,

'I couldn't stop crying as I was making it. It was a good way of acknowledging what I missed about the past: the picnics, Jake learning to walk again after a long spell in hospital, the kids camping in the garden. Now Nick and I want to make him a leaving-home quilt, a bit like the "Wandering Turkey" quilts made by American pioneers to give to children when they left home to marry. There was also a lovely tradition in England that parents would design a quilt together for a groom to take to his bride. I had this idea that I could write little messages and put them inside – it would allow me to say slightly cheesy things that my son wouldn't be able to read! I wasn't sure if Jake would want it, but I asked him and he said he would love it.

'I am also planning a weekend away with three old friends who are also empty nesters, who live at opposite ends of the country. When Jake left I wanted someone to be a witness to the parent I had been and to celebrate that, as well as recognising the poignancy of him going. That gave me the idea of spending a weekend with friends, so that we could tell the story of our parenting. I did a storytelling course for my forty-ninth birthday, and wrote a story for Maud when she went to Canada. Now I would like to write something about my experiences as a parent.'

Birthdays

Cultural and religious rituals, such as christenings and bar mitzvahs, are important ways of publicly marking the key transitions in the lives of parents and children. Eighteenth birthdays have taken on extra significance since it became the official marker of legal adulthood. They offer an obvious opportunity to celebrate the past as well as to wish luck for the future. Heather came up with an unusual addition: a leaving-home ceremony which was held on the day before her daughter Ishbel's eighteenth birthday party. She hired a yurt – quite a sight in a suburban Scottish back garden! – and invited the small group of friends and relatives who had played an important part in Ishbel's upbringing. It was clearly important that her daughter was keen on the idea too.

The preparations took place over several weeks and inspired the whole family to reflect both on the past and the future.

'Ishbel's eighteenth felt like a significant birthday, and it was also shortly before she went travelling, which felt like a big thing for all of us. We had all brought Ishbel small tokens, which we attached to a door-hanging during the ceremony: my mother, for example, brought her some beads she had loved as a child. Ishbel had also made everyone a gift, which she gave to each of us in turn. It was an opportunity for her to say thank you. Then the friend who was leading the ceremony asked Ishbel to sit between Andy and I. She tied a thread around our wrists and told Ishbel to cut it when she was ready. It was terribly emotional for me and lots of people were crying. But there was a lot of laughter and singing too. Going through that whole process – preparing for it as well as the ceremony itself – was very therapeutic for me, and it made it much easier for me when she left.'

A leaving-home ceremony in a yurt wouldn't suit everyone – Heather is the first to admit that, and she took great pains to put the guests at their ease; however, the ceremony incorporated a number of ideas which other parents could find helpful in other, more private, contexts. Their value lies in focusing attention on the past and the future, and offering ways to acknowledge the significance of children leaving and to talk about and explore different issues.

For example, Heather wrote her daughter a letter. Like many parents she had thought about it for some time, but had never got round to putting pen to paper. She also made Ishbel two gifts, which were further opportunities for reflection: 'I said things in the letter which I'd been wanting to say to her for years – the things I would want her to know if I died tomorrow,' she explains.

> 'I wrote about her very young childhood and the things I'd loved doing with her. I suppose they are the kinds of things parents might say on their child's wedding day, but I was glad I said them just before she left home.
>
> 'As I was making the gifts, I thought carefully about what I was making and why. One was a finger labyrinth made out of clay, which was a way of saying, "If you ever feel lost, I hope this will help you to find your way home, both to us and to your inner self." I also made her a doll – a kind of talisman to take on her journey. I got the idea from the Russian folk tale called "Vasilisa the Beautiful", about a mother who gave her daughter a small doll and told her that if she was ever in trouble it would help her. I read Ishbel the story with her young nieces after I gave her the doll. Of course, I didn't really believe it would protect her, but there was something very therapeutic about making something that was supposed to do that. It's by her bed at university and I know it's really precious to her.'

Support

There is little doubt that other parents' experiences of the empty nest can put your own in perspective, and help to make sense of conflicting emotions. Yet it is striking how many parents feel isolated in this respect: women with no shortage of friends said they found it hard to find other women who really understood their point of view, who weren't just depressing and negative about the empty nest. Perhaps this is simply because it is ultimately a very personal experience. Whatever the reason, it means that many women swallow the myth that everyone else is sailing through fine, thanks to their apparently perfect busy lives and supportive partners.

Women don't want to admit to missing their kids now that there is so much pressure to be fulfilled in every corner of life, and so much status comes from paid work. It feels like failure, an indication that they need to get a life beyond children. Too often, mothers who are utterly bereft are made to feel they have brought it on themselves by being too involved with their kids and that they need to get a life. The family therapist, Kate Daniels, says, 'I find that a lot of parents continually labour with fantasies that everyone else is doing things much better. It's curious how many people I see who think they're the only ones getting things wrong and everyone else is getting things right. In our society we allow for young mothers to talk about their experiences in groups. We accommodate and tacitly give permission for certain things to be discussed communally, but other things we don't. While it is true that the empty nest is talked about more, I don't know how much this idea of people having supportive conversations with each other about their children leaving is encouraged or allowed for.'

TIPS
Finding space to take stock

- A creative course offers new outlets to explore and express your feelings.
- Learn to meditate or join a yoga class.

- Hypnotherapy. A good hypnotherapist can help break habits and facilitate focus: many offer recordings to consolidate the effect.
- A long walk or a day by the sea, alone or with a friend.
- A weekend away or a retreat.
- Get into the habit of writing a diary – it doesn't have to be every day – or a scrapbook of memorabilia with captions.

Informal support networks

Support groups for empty nesters don't exist, but perhaps they should. There are plenty of opportunities for younger mothers to socialise with their babies and toddlers, and air problems through social networks like the National Childbirth Trust and Internet parenting forums, and this continues through primary school. But this kind of friendly support – which isn't problem-centred but allows problems to be aired as part of general chatting – dries up as your kids get older. It's not hard to see why. The idea of an empty nesters' club or a group for parents of teenagers sounds so negative; it doesn't have quite the same appeal. Yet parents of older children – whether they are teenagers or leaving home – would often welcome informal contexts to talk about the changing relationships in their family and with their partner, and their complex emotions. Above all, they need to feel they are not alone.

Instead, a network of informal support has quietly grown up under a different guise: book clubs, allotments, craft workshops, dancing sessions, walking groups, evening classes. These are not targeted at empty nesters, and attract all ages, but they still offer informal opportunities to chat about what people are going through. My sons' old school runs a former parents' group, which draws in members by organising really great courses and events. This means that men and women go because they're interested in the subject, not because they're actively seeking support. Opportunities to talk about your stage in life arise quite naturally, without feeling forced.

The same thing happens when people are focused on making things together. Even apparently shy women open up when they are concentrating alongside each other: perhaps the lack of direct eye contact is liberating. Craft workshops and knitting groups go some way towards filling the void left by the consciousness-raising groups of the 1970s, which made women realise they weren't alone in their feelings and frustrations. That might be overegging the pudding, but it is one explanation for the huge resurgence of interest in communal crafting, which is surely to do with much more than a desire to learn new skills.

TIPS
Practical ways to take stock

- Compile an album of photographs and mementoes of significant transitions in your child's life – the perfect birthday or leaving present.
- Mark your child's departure with a celebration which acknowledges its significance. It could be small and personal, or involve family and/or friends.
- Write a letter to your child about your life together. It will prompt memories and offer an opportunity to reflect, even if you don't send it straight away.
- Make something simple out of your children's old clothes: a cushion cover, a collage, a piece of patchwork, a rag-rug.

Chapter 10

A New Direction

'She wrenched herself away from the contemplation of all
the dreary changes that would be brought about to herself
by her son's marriage; she forced her thoughts into the
accustomed household grooves . . . Still he did not come.
Doubtless he was with Miss Hale. The new love was
displacing her already from her place as first in his heart.
A terrible pain – a pang of vain jealousy – shot through
her: she hardly knew whether it was more physical or
mental; but it forced her to sit down.'

North and South by Elizabeth Gaskell

Life inevitably takes a different course when children leave,
so it is a natural juncture to make other changes too. Parents
who move on themselves and actively instigate change in
their own lives avoid the uncomfortable feeling that they've
been left behind by their kids. It also helps to establish a
more balanced relationship with adult children, because
you're not hanging on their every move or living your life
through them.

But the notion that from now on anything is possible feels
both exciting and overwhelming. Those familiar stories of
people who totally change tack in midlife – accountants who
become dairy farmers, and so on – are inspiring, and this
chapter ends with two dramatic life changes. But they can
be daunting too. The idea that you could move house, change

careers, retrain, travel, volunteer, do a degree or learn to fly is enough to make anyone want to crawl back under the duvet. In fact, less dramatic changes can be just as significant and equally rewarding.

A new direction is much more to do with a shift of attitude, a new way of thinking about life with you, and no longer the children, at its centre. Children will always be a priority, but they are no longer the main driving force. This creates a dilemma: parents still want to be there for their kids, to remain closely involved and to help in a crisis, but at times this conflicts with attempts to build a life beyond the family. Factoring adult children into your arrangements while not allowing your whole life to revolve around them is a difficult balancing act, and at times parents face tough decisions. Of course, it is a shame if you're trekking in Nepal when they decide to drop in, but there will be other opportunities to see them. Your life has its own new direction too, and sometimes you just have to stick with it and live with the occasional regret.

A new direction at home

Before parents can move on they need to think about breaking habits that are embedded in every area of family life, from daily routines to ways of thinking about our own potential. Practical adjustments seem trivial but feel loaded. The family therapist, Kate Daniels, admits, 'I used to stand in Sainsbury's and think, *I don't need this trolley, I need a basket.* And I'd feel sad that I didn't have to buy the food my son liked any more, and end up buying it anyway.'

Ditching habits that are no longer relevant also helps parents miss their children less. When children leave, the timetable of the week – and indeed the year – goes out of the window, and if parents remain stuck in child-at-home mode the gaps in the routine are more obvious and more painful. So, the parent who still unconsciously waits for the doorbell at four o'clock, or focuses their plans on the college vacations, is likely to feel more miserable than the parent who has found other fish to fry.

However, because even the dullest domestic routines can be curiously comforting, they can be hard to let go. You might think it would be a relief not having to pluck wet towels from bedroom floors or stay sober in case someone needs a lift, but those things provide a structure which parents can feel lost without. Rustling up a snack after school, or giving someone a lift, are intrinsic to nurturing children. So, rather than casting aside domestic burdens enthusiastically, many parents, like Charlie, a single working father of two daughters, find them hard to let go:

'It was rather lovely having all the day-to-day stuff to do, like cooking and the weekly shop. I found it very reassuring and I missed it when my daughters left. The fact that you're not needed on a day-to-day basis – that's where your emptiness is. You have to find a way of filling that time, which is a big adjustment. But when you get used to it it's also quite nice not to be needed so much, not to be responsible. There is a positive side to no longer having to worry whether there is food in the cupboard, not having to think about cooking and all those practical things – that is hugely liberating. Suddenly you find all this time you never had before.

'But it also meant I had to think about me, and that was not so groovy, actually. It's easier to have a life with children, where you aren't having to think about what you're doing for yourself. When they were at home I never had to worry about how I was doing, I could just put all my energies into my kids. Thinking about what I'm doing for myself is much harder and more complex, and I'd rather not, I'd rather think about them. When they went I had to think about me and it was a shock, because I didn't really know what my purpose was any more. I didn't really know what I wanted to do with my life for me.'

Women who have been out of the workforce

Similar uncertainties haunt many women who gave up work to raise their kids and feel undecided about getting back into the workforce. Chloe says,

> 'For the last few years it's been quite strange, feeling like I really need something meaningful to do if the children don't need me. If I'm not busy enough I tend to be too concerned about issues in the girls' lives and start to live through them. I had wondered about retraining. I long to focus on one thing at a time, to do something properly. I like trying new things and I quite like the challenge. But it feels slightly late to be starting a career, and to find yourself working alongside 18-year-olds when you're 50. And up till now I haven't felt I've got any brain time to really think about it – my brain feels addled.'

Women who have been out of the workforce have huge advantages: they're ready and raring for change and when they find the right direction they're likely to have more energy and enthusiasm than someone who has been plugging away in the same job for years. We're often told that managing a home and family develops highly desirable skills, and it's true, according to Cary Cooper, Distinguished Professor of Organisational Psychology and Health at Lancaster University Management School: 'Women have all the social and interpersonal skills needed in a lot of jobs, by virtue of their experience at home, which is essentially a managerial role. And the mothering role trains women to be very adaptable and flexible. But because they're older they may not be self-confident and they may worry that they're not as good as younger people who have all these computer skills and so on. Our experience at universities bears this out: students who take degrees later in life almost always do better than younger students, because they really are motivated. Yet they all think they are not going to do so well.'

This lack of confidence plagues women who have been out of the workforce and adds to the feeling of uncertainty about what happens next. Many of the stay-at-home mothers I interviewed underestimated their skills, even when they had several enterprising strings to their bow; for example, Heather, who is quoted below, is a voluntary director of a parenting charity, teaches children to sew and has a small jewellery business. Yet perhaps because what they do is casual, often home-based and sometimes unpaid, women wrongly feel that it somehow doesn't count as 'real' work. In fact full-time mothers who have explored their own interests in the years when their parenting commitments begin to tail off are in a strong position to find work that more than fills the gap. They have already explored what they find fulfilling; now it's a question of working out how that might transfer to paid employment.

Step back – don't rush

Professor Cooper emphasises the importance of taking time out to consider the next stage. He advises, 'Whatever you do, don't rush on to the next thing. The empty nest is a perfect opportunity to take stock and do an assessment of yourself, to think through what options are open to you. It's a definitive point at which you can say, "Now I can get on with my life." But then you have to ask yourself, "What is my life, what do I want to do with the next 30 or 40 years?"'

Case Study: Heather

Heather, who gave up teaching to home-educate her two daughters, began exploring the various options she could pursue in the year before her younger daughter, Emily, started college. Like many full-time parents she needed a breathing

space, and when I interviewed her a few months before her
daughter was due to start college she said,

> 'I feel like I've had a 20-year reprieve from facing difficult
> questions about my career. I don't yet feel I've got the
> mental space to think about what to do next. I've given
> myself 100 per cent to being a mother and home educator
> and although I've loved it there were times when I felt I had
> completely lost sight of myself. So my plan now is to use
> Emily's first term as my time, to take a breather and see
> what comes up. I feel I need some time to think more
> creatively about myself and what I really want to do next.
> If I can identify what my goal is, I feel pretty confident that
> I'll find a way of achieving it. I'm planning to take a similar
> approach as I took to my daughters' education: look at my
> interests and develop them. And find ways of earning money
> doing things that I genuinely enjoy. One of my big loves has
> always been craft, and recently I've started sewing classes
> for children as a way of carving out time to get back into
> that.
>
> 'I don't particularly want to go back to full-time teaching,
> but I'm not qualified to do anything else. I could retrain and
> do something completely different but what would that be?
> I'm trying very hard to be positive about the children leaving
> home, but it's an effort and sometimes I do feel weary and
> middle-aged. But I don't enjoy sitting around and I don't
> want to slide into early retirement.'

When I spoke to Heather a few weeks after Emily started
college she sounded much more positive; clearly giving herself
time to think creatively about which areas of her life to
develop had paid off. She says,

> 'I must admit I'm absolutely loving the space it's giving me.
> I'm almost feeling "on top of things" for the first time in
> years and I'm also beginning to get some creative ideas

for what I want to do both now and in the future. I feel much less weary and middle-aged! I went on a "Goals" course for people who have been unemployed for a while run by my local council, which was interesting and helpful. I made some new friends and found out about adult literacy tutor training, something I'm considering doing. It also led on to my finding a "veg growing" mentor as part of my lifelong dream of having a smallholding (which may not happen, but I'm still working towards it!).'

Boredom and guilt

The home-based mother's biggest enemy is boredom. Too much time on your hands can be as paralysing as never having enough. Women are stuck between a rock and a hard place: they need to take time to work out what to do next, but the less they do the less confident they may become. Georgia Foster, a hypnotherapist and author of several books on breaking habits, says, 'Boredom is often underestimated; it is incredibly stressful. When you're bored you think too much and worry too much. If you've got too much time on your hands the inner critic comes into play and everything becomes worse than it is. So I think women need to find something – not necessarily a paid or permanent job – that is going to stimulate them. That is a really big ask, particularly if someone has been out of the workforce for a long time and may have self-esteem issues. They may not feel confident about locating the resources within themselves to change or improve their lives.

'Many women whose lives have until now been so busy looking after and thinking about other people feel incredibly guilty when they realise they have all this time on their hands. They feel that they should be more productive, get a job, do something constructive with their time. The guilt is really strong: their inner-critic says you've got this golden opportunity to move on in your life, what's wrong with you?

Small but significant steps towards change are usually better than rushing into a total change of direction.'

When it comes to going back into the workforce, or changing career, Professor Cooper advises, 'I would start by thinking through your competencies and what you really want to do, whether you need training and how much. And then map it out. If you are really unsure you could have aptitude testing with an occupational psychologist; you don't have to go along with all their conclusions, but it just tells you something about your capabilities and personality. Then you can look at occupations that fit: you may find something you've never thought of. I would then trial it by shadowing someone in that job. By doing that you may find out that it's not exactly what you thought, or that it really is what you want to do. Women at this stage may also need to build up their confidence, perhaps by taking a refresher course, particularly if you are going to do something very different from what you did before, but even if you are going back to the same job.'

Short residential courses or volunteer breaks are a way of dipping a toe in the water without having to make a long-term commitment, as well as a way of broadening the mind. A course – not necessarily related to the area you are thinking of pursuing – a holiday or a retreat all allow you to step outside the routines of daily life and take an objective look at possibilities. Removed from the mental clutter of daily life, the mind can quieten and allow in new ideas about the future. It can also be a natural way of making a clean break with old habits; you come home refreshed and ready to make a fresh start. It's important to be daring as well as realistic and remember that if something turns out to be a dead end it is still productive in its own way. As in so many areas of life, you may have to kiss a lot of frogs before you find your handsome prince – or in this case, a fulfilling new occupation.

When Nina took a three-month sabbatical from her

part-time job after her two daughters left, it radically changed her plans for the future. She spent most of the time travelling in South America.

> 'When I got back to my job I realised I was a bit bored with it, and I wanted my brain to be sharpened up a bit. So I started looking into possibilities for when I retired, maybe in about five years' time, which would be closer to my life-long interest in development studies, refugee issues and so on. I was quite surprised to discover that a minimum of an MA in Human Rights was required for a voluntary post I saw advertised at Médecins Sans Frontières. So I decided to take an MA part-time. I completely freaked out in the first term because I'm at least 20 years older than everyone else, but I just love it. I can't tell you how much I've learned. This is the area I should have been working in all my life really, but I got sidetracked by motherhood. I've started doing something I always meant to do and that feels great, and since I started studying, my attitude to my job has changed and I'm enjoying it much more. It's a bit of a financial dip, because I had to give up one of my two part-time jobs, but it's definitely worth it. It's one of many ways of filling the gap the girls have left.'

Can work prevent empty nest syndrome?

Interesting occupations and a busy life undoubtedly make the absence of children easier to bear. Of course, working mothers still miss their kids, but they don't confront the yawning hole in their daily routine or the lack of purpose which hits home-based mothers. If you go out to work, the kids' physical absence is not in your face, at least during the day. Meanwhile, work offers another dimension to your identity, an alternative reference point; at work people see you first as a colleague, not as a parent (even if you can't stop talking about the kids!). It can be particularly reassuring when the kids first leave to slot straight into a ready-made life beyond the family.

Being freelance myself I know very well that I miss the kids much less and feel better about the empty nest when I have tight deadlines. Women who work full-time generally agree. Linda, a primary school teacher, says,

'I was very worried about my daughter going away, because she had spent her gap year having treatment for cancer. She was determined to start university at the right time, but it was quite scary and I felt she was very vulnerable. Of course, I still worried, and I rang her every day, but because I have quite a demanding job, leaving at seven and getting home at six, there wasn't much time to miss her, or even be aware that the nest was totally empty. Teaching at my age is quite exhausting and I've got plenty of distractions through work and through friends.'

Liz, a single parent, embarked on a new full-time career the day after she dropped her 19-year-old daughter Laura, who has Down's Syndrome, at her new residential college. Her son, Jack, left for Canada at around the same time.

'Overnight I went from being a full-on carer to a full-time job that took every inch of my energy, because I didn't have a degree and felt I had to prove myself. I didn't really miss the children because the job stretched me and developed a whole new side to my life. Without it I would have worried about Laura much more, just because I had the time to. I don't know how women who don't work manage when their children leave.'

A new direction for working mothers

Contrary to popular myth, the empty nest may have an equally significant impact on the lives of working mothers.

Gone is that tension of needing to be in two places at the same time, and in its place comes a new single-mindedness and focus. Cambridge University psychologist, Terri Apter, explains, 'When you are at work, a lot of your mind is on the fact that your child is going to be home at five and has an exam tomorrow, or she's lonely so you'd better try to get back. You're still thinking about all of these things even when they're 17. So, your child being away from home makes quite a difference. You may find you have a lot more energy.' Women who are used to constantly juggling work and family now feel free to pursue their careers without feeling guilty. Women who turned down career opportunities because they put their children first – that's most of us – can from now on seize them. And while previous generations of women were expected to fit their plans around their husbands', even after the kids had gone, these days, hopefully, partners are more inclined to negotiate and compromise with each other.

Age makes a difference in some professions more than others, but what really counts is attitude. Judy was in her early fifties when, after being a more or less full-time mother to her five kids for nearly 30 years, she embarked on a new career and founded the UK Jewish Film Festival when her youngest, Haia, was eight. She began by working part-time from home, and only went full-time when Haia went to university two years ago, by which time Judy had turned 60. Judy says,

'I feel like I've been let out of school. Before Haia left home I was forever clock-watching, not going to work-related things I ought to have been at because I wanted to be there when Haia came home. I wanted to be with her, being a mummy, but at the same time there was a pull to other things. I never resented it, but it really gave me a lot of anguish. So, what I've experienced since she left is a real sense of relief, an enormous release. I'm able to be more available for my work and I'm very lucky in that I love what I do and I am aware that that is a real luxury.

'Having a new career late in life certainly helped me to cope with the empty nest. I was certainly aware of my maternal role in life changing, but I felt ready. I think that I was very lucky, because the timing suited me and I don't know if I would have been able to let Haia go in quite the same way if I hadn't had a career that I love. But finding that new focus wasn't intentional, it just happened at the right time.'

A seven-year study for the Economic and Social Research Council in the 1990s found that women in their mid-forties enjoyed better jobs, higher self-esteem and better family relationships than younger women. The strongest change for the better was usually work related; that was the time that many women were promoted, began courses in higher education or started their own businesses. If the timing is right, the empty nest enables women to consolidate the successes and experiences of the previous years. This was certainly true for Anne, a designer who worked part-time while her two children were growing up. A single parent, she recently moved cities to take up a full-time job.

'I really felt that this was the time for me to seize opportunities. The kids have gone; you have to move on too, don't you? I was offered a full-time post a year after my daughter went to university. There was suddenly so much more space – emotionally, intellectually, time-wise. I can't understand why, because it wasn't that I had been doing much for her, and she wasn't at all demanding.

'I originally went freelance over 20 years ago, just before Jess was born, and I always steered my work in a particular direction to fit in with the kids. So this new job, which is a big step forward career-wise, has come at the perfect time. It's a complete change of fortune financially. After the

insecurity of freelancing for years, and claiming Child Tax
Credit, I have the security of a good salary. It was also very
attractive to be sent to a new city, because I wanted to
move, and otherwise how do you decide where you move
to? Talk about a new beginning!'

The downside is that women still have to juggle family
commitments: not only adult kids who still need support but
also ailing parents – yet often with less understanding from
the boss. From now on demands are less predictable: suddenly
you have to drop everything to sort out a crisis. Cambridge
University psychologist, Terri Apter, says, 'The sandwich
generation is a big thing for women: it has a profound impact
on women's work in midlife. Sometimes you still have to
make very tough decisions about what is going to come first
– your career or your family. When women have young kids,
employers understand, and there are family-friendly policies
they have to abide by, whereas they don't always understand
problems with adult kids and elderly parents. Now women
may have to deal with an adult child having a bad three
months in between jobs or if he unexpectedly fails an exam,
and that means re-thinking everything. And you don't know
when there's going to be an emergency until it happens.'

Work–life balance still matters

Throwing yourself into working all the hours God gives is
a tempting option, particularly for professional women
whose careers have been on the back burner for years. That's
fine if it's what you really want, but not so good if you just
get into a rut of working harder because you can't think
what else to do. There is a wealth of alternatives: you could
change tack completely, work less, go freelance, start a business. Work–life balance is still important, even when the
family isn't around.

Keeping a balance is at the forefront of Philippa's mind.

She has combined a career in the NHS with motherhood for 35 years, having had the first of her three children at the age of 22. Unlike most mothers, she has never had the experience of coming home from work and only having herself to think about. She says,

'I'm lucky that although I've always put the children first it hasn't held me back in my career, and now I could make much more of my working life. I've got a range of possibilities: I could take on more responsibilities, do research or go into private practice. But there are other things outside work which are really important to me and which I want to develop before I die – or before I have grandchildren: I would love to take a degree in art history or music. And recently I've been reminded of how deeply pleasurable I used to find sewing and making clothes, so I'd like to do more of that. My husband and I are also planning to move to the country, and although we would both carry on working, that would open up a range of other possibilities too.'

One way to prevent work taking over is to impose your own limits on the working week to replace the structure of family demands: if you take work home, set limits on how long you spend on it. Amira, an academic, has revamped her schedules now that her son's and daughter's needs no longer put a cap on the time she can spend at work. She explains,

'My job expands to fill whatever time is available – it's never finished, there's always plenty to do, and it's largely self-generated. Because I control everything myself, I used to welcome the fact that my daughter's school timetable drove mine. Since she left I've been trying to build in strategies at work to manage the home–work balance so that I don't get sucked into working at weekends and in the evenings. My husband often has evening meetings and when there isn't anyone at home it's tempting to spend yet another evening on revisions. So I'm making sure I arrange social commitments which make that less inevitable.'

Working from home: new patterns

Parents who work from home may also need to impose a different structure on the working week. It may be the perfect solution when the children are younger but when there's no one bursting through the door at 4.00 p.m. to break up the routine, it can feel isolated and lonely. I speak from the heart!

If you have no choice but to work from home, it should be possible to build in sociable activities to break up the day, or even find part-time work or volunteering to complement the more solitary days. When work had to fit around school runs and meals, the natural tendency is to rush lunch and keep social phone calls to a minimum. Now it's perfectly possible – indeed it will almost certainly make you more productive – to meet people for lunch or tea, and to set aside time to chat to friends on the phone. Being more sociable in your spare time could also help.

When Janet saw the empty nest approaching she looked for new ways of working outside the home; having experienced a bout of depression in the past she wanted to reduce the risk of it recurring. Her work had always been organised around being a mum, and when her son and daughter were young she gave up social work to do desktop publishing from home.

'When it was coming up to Susannah leaving I decided that I needed to find work outside the home, so I trained for mediation, which is what I do now. Moving out of the home, finding work that I enjoyed and mixing with people I liked mitigated the sense of loss; however, one thing I go through periodically is a sense that I could have done better. When

the children left there was a feeling that this was an opportunity for change, but there was a "but", a feeling that in
many ways I was too old to rise to it adequately. I was 50,
but I just didn't have that singular motivation to make a
huge change.'

Making changes

Hobbies and volunteering

Previous generations of empty nest women filled their days
with unpaid activities: volunteering, gardening, hobbies,
meeting friends. Expectations of what makes for a fulfilling
life are so much grander now, and women who choose to fill
their days with unpaid activity are made to feel a bit light-
weight. Hobbies and volunteering just aren't valued in the
same way as unpaid work, although attitudes are changing.
It's not just about saving money; alongside the revival of
interest in volunteering and pride in the local community,
allotments, dressmaking and choirs are acquiring a new cachet.
Activities that are initially taken up grudgingly as a consolation
for loss, and a way of filling the empty hours, can rapidly
develop into sources of genuine pleasure and fulfilment. And
new interests may lead to bigger things. We've all heard of
women who started doing yoga and ended up training to teach
it themselves, or turned a weekend interest in gardening or
decorating into a professional business. Rona, for example,
took up sailing as a way of meeting people after her divorce
and ended up sailing round the world (see page 195).

Should you get a dog?

Empty nesters often talk about finding a new outlet for their
nurturing side, which remains a driving force long after it
has served its purpose with the kids. Suddenly, it becomes
clear why middle-aged people buy dogs and love gardening.

But caution is advisable when it comes to buying a dog – or getting chickens or keeping bees – because the urge may well wear off as you get used to more freedom and find other stuff to do. There's no doubt that a dog adds a whole new dimension to life; it's just what some people need. But it would be a shame to be stuck with some new commitment that offers convenient excuses not to travel or move, or seize new opportunities. Julia is forthright: 'The dog is Mike's baby and she is very irritating and intensely intrusive. I call her PK: "Passion Killer". We have all this wonderful free time now, but you still have to think of the dog. She is a complication – not advisable in the empty nest.'

For many women the need to nurture persists, and it becomes the focus of new careers. Clare has found huge satisfaction as a teacher of t'ai chi and painting. She now uses the latter in rehabilitation work with women prisoners – a direction she never imagined she would go in. She says,

'When the kids first left I found myself looking at dogs in the park and thinking how nice it would be to have one. Then I thought, *Hang on a minute, the last thing I need now is a child replacement.* I feel like I've been caring for people long enough: not just my children but my mother too. I don't really want to be needed any more. But at the same time I've realised that I would like to find a new direction for my nurturing side.

'Now the part of me which became empty when the children moved out is filling up as I find other ways of mothering myself and others. I think the deep connections you have with your children open you up to be able to love and care for other people generally. Both the teacher and the mother in me wants to nurture others.'

Chloe, who moved back to the UK after spending most of her married life working in the developing world, also wants to find more permanent channels for her nurturing skills:

'I've come to the conclusion that if I can't overcome these urges I should at least find something useful to nurture. This morning I thought, *This is ridiculous, I'm nurturing these cosmos seedlings as if they were human beings.* I suddenly see why middle-aged people are gardeners; it's displacement nurturing. We're all out there, tidying the garden because we can't tidy our families any more. It makes me think it's time for us to move overseas again; I would rather be somewhere out in Africa running an orphanage than spending the rest of my life nurturing this house. That would feel like quite a waste.'

Fitting your new direction around the kids

Making plans and developing a new direction often conflicts with children's often chaotic and last-minute plans. Of course, parents want to be around when a child comes home, but waiting for them to decide what they're doing can be frustrating. There are times when it feels pointless trying to make your own arrangements, because you always seem to be away when they want to visit, or you have to drop everything if they need support in a crisis. And when they do come home you barely see them, because they spend most of the time out with their mates. Mark still isn't quite used to putting his own plans on hold until his daughter, Catherine, makes up her mind. He says,

'I desperately want to see Catherine over the summer, but she is non-committal. It's not that she doesn't want to come and see me, it's just her life; she has her own plans. It can be quite frustrating to think that my whole summer holiday depends on the decisions of some 20-year-old friend of hers who she is travelling with, and that's her priority. Or her boyfriend's plans dictate her arrangements and therefore affect me, because it means she can only come here for three days at Easter or whatever. That's just a bit sad.'

Meanwhile, when the empty nest arrives, many parents find themselves wondering what happened to all the free time they had anticipated. They are just as busy, either with work or new commitments. But, for other parents, 'me-time' – the holy grail for parents of young children – has a hollow ring. It is common for parents in the thick of family life to take up solitary pastimes to get away, to find a bit of peace. But after years trying to squeeze space for yourself, me-time has arrived in bucketloads, and it has lost its appeal. Once the kids have gone so does the need to go looking for peace, and it can get a bit lonely.

Patrick, a single father, had always been a keen sailor and he took up rowing when his sons were old enough to look after themselves.

'Since I've been living on my own I have become aware that I'm doing all these activities that are solitary. I don't really want to spend so much time by myself. I started rowing when the kids were old enough for me to do something on my own, for me. It was my first foray into "me-time" and it felt like such a relief to do something on my own; it was great to be solitary when you were spending every moment of the day thinking about the kids and doing things with them. Then, when the kids leave, you think, *Actually, I don't want to do all these things on my own, I'm on my own too much*.

'Then about four years ago I bought a really high perform-ance sailing boat – it was the equivalent of buying a Porsche in a midlife crisis – which I used to sail by myself. I nearly sold it after a week, because it was such a handful. I'm probably never going to completely master it, because I've realised that sailing by myself is a very lonely pastime, and I can't join a club because of work schedules.'

It may be time to re-think how you spend your spare time, bearing in mind that there may be activities you once loved but had to put on hold because of lack of time or mental space. Top of my list are long walks (the kids used to moan); playing the flute (the kids interrupted when they were little and I got out of the habit). Through the children you may also have discovered all sorts of new interests: bike riding, perhaps? Drawing and painting? Body boarding? And then there are things you've always wanted to do but never got the chance. For me it's learning to ride a horse and learning the cha-cha.

Finding your flow

Parents now have a golden opportunity to rediscover that wonderful feeling of losing yourself in the moment, known as 'flow'. You could also call it 'fun', if that didn't conjure up images of forced jollity and 1950s holiday camps. It's something many parents have lost sight of among all the myriad stresses of bringing up kids, organising a household and working. Although it may take a bit of effort to discover it, once found it feels blissfully effortless. It is in anything you find truly absorbing, which engages your strengths and abilities and uses them in a way that resonates with who you are. For one person that might involve a very physical pursuit, such as abseiling or cycling, whereas for someone else it could be basket-weaving or learning a language.

Ultimately, the changes parents make are a matter of individual choice. The empty nest is a chance to find out what fulfilment means to us. This is rarely just to do with success at work and it is often an intermingling of several different strands in our personal lives. An element of acceptance combines with regret for past opportunities you can no longer take up, for things that haven't been. Charlie says,

'Some people make me feel I should face up to myself and look at what I'm doing in terms of fulfilment. But I have had fulfilment in other ways: I'm closer to my daughters than ever before and I love looking after my grandchild. It fulfils something in me again. I don't know what it is – escapism probably. I would like to have another go at what I started out doing: trying to be an artist. But now I've got loads of reasons why not to again. I like to escape from myself. But I would say I am a pretty fulfilled person.'

Leave home yourself

Gap years are becoming increasingly popular among the baby boomer generation. Leaving home yourself for a few months or even longer is a defiant way of sticking two fingers up to the empty nest; it is also one way of exploring new interests and passions. The next two women – both traditional, home-based mothers – chose adventurous challenges that propelled their lives in radically new directions. Neither of the women had done anything like it before: Pen took up long-distance cycling, while Rona sailed around the world. Pen used to cycle with her daughters, while Rona joined a sailing club in her forties to meet people after her divorce. Their experiences are inspiring, because even if most of us would never contemplate such extreme adventures, they illustrate how taking on a new challenge can open up new opportunities which you might never have thought of before. There are all sorts of ways of stretching yourself: you don't have to go around the world to do it. They also illustrate that while a break with domesticity is fantastically liberating, it is impossible to leave parental responsibilities behind completely.

Case Study: Pen

Pen was in her early fifties when the youngest of her four daughters went on her gap year to Central Africa and she did her first three-month cycle trip across America.

'When my daughter left I suddenly thought, *Wow, they've all gone, I'm going to leave too.* It was a really great opportunity, and I grabbed it. I'd been around with kids growing up for ages because my oldest daughter was born when I was 24, my youngest when I was 41. She left in February and I set off in May. The first trip was a complete eye-opener and it changed my life. It tested me in ways I had never been tested as a mother, and tested things I had never thought wanted testing. Until then it had never crossed my mind that I would really enjoy the physical challenge, being totally exhausted with your back against the wall, and in a foreign area you've never been to before. I usually bike on my own, which is quite nerve-racking too. You stretch yourself as far as you can stretch – both mentally and physically.

'And the great thing is that it takes you right away from domesticity. I reckon it takes me at least three weeks to completely let go. When I set off I'm in quite a highly strung, nervous state and it takes a long time to wind down and let go and to realise that you're no longer thinking about what's happening back home. It's nice not to be able to communicate too much. At times I used to ask myself, "Am I really enjoying this? Do I really like being on my own?" On the whole I did, because you have total freedom. There is nobody else to consider, you are completely self-sufficient. You only think about what you want: you can go where you want to, stop where you want to. What I love most is that it's very good thinking time, sitting on a saddle for seven hours a day. It's slightly like being on a retreat where you can really work things out. I found I really enjoyed that – in fact it became almost addictive; all this time and space just to think.

'It's enabled me to be better about letting my daughters go and allowing them to have their own lives. Of course, it was hard at times. On that first bike ride I had no way of contacting my youngest daughter in Central Africa for the

six weeks when she was travelling around too. I remember
thinking that it's like she's gone round to the back of the
moon, like the first spaceship which went out of contact
while on the dark side of the moon. I was very concerned
about how she was getting on so that was quite a difficult
time.'

Pen never looked back; on her return to Scotland she
embarked on another totally new departure, an Open
University degree in Humanities. Since then she has alter-
nated long-distance solo bike rides, which often raise
money for charity, with her degree. Now in her seventies
she is planning her next big ride for charity around Lake
Victoria.

Round-the-world yachtswoman, Rona Cant, also faced
huge anxieties about leaving her son and daughter, as well
as her own ability to cope at sea for ten months. She had
only started sailing five years earlier, and at 51 was the oldest
woman on the 32,000-mile BT Global Challenge. She set
off while her son, Simon, was on his gap year, and had to
ask her daughter, Nicola, to settle him into university.

'It was really, really tough, that leaving: I went back on to
the quay four times to say goodbye and we were all crying
our eyes out. I stood on the deck thinking, *Why am I doing
this?* I was really upset, and I was aware that people –
especially my mother – thought I was being selfish to leave
my children. But at the end of the day it was the best thing
I could have done for them and for me. I'd really had enough
of people telling me what to do. I felt this is my time now
and it's lovely. Having said that, I did feel very much that it
was my job to settle Simon into university and I was really
sad that I wasn't there for him for his first year. He split
up with a girlfriend that Christmas and I felt I should have
been there. But sometimes you can't be and you just have
to accept that it's tough. And I'm sure it made them stronger.'

An ocean-going racing yacht sounds like the last place to channel nurturing skills, but Rona soon found she had a dual role:

> 'Part of my job was to be mum in case any of the younger ones got homesick – which happened a lot at Christmas. It was very odd having two personas: sailor and nurturer. There were two things running in parallel: it was, I'm free, I'm away, I've got no one I need to look after – except the other 17 people on this yacht, I've got to help keep them safe.
>
> 'If I hadn't had the break, I could very possibly have gone mad. When I was married I was living the life I thought I ought to lead, and not the life I really wanted to lead. The Global Challenge forced me to do new things. There was no time to mourn the children leaving home because I was so involved with the preparation: during Simon's gap year I missed him dreadfully, but it freed me to train and work on the yacht before we set sail. I didn't have to worry about him being at home saying, "Mum where are you?" That was really good for both of us. I had never wanted to be one of those mothers who is always ringing their kids at uni. I think it helped them as well that I wasn't around so much, because I used to do everything for them and I was always there. Suddenly, they had to fend for themselves and they had to make it work.'

Rona had always felt that marriage had held her back, and this was the first opportunity since her divorce to do something for herself. She used to be a part-time secretary; now she runs her own business as a motivational speaker. She says, 'The Global Challenge changed me completely; it gave me an astronomical sense of achievement. I'm far more confident now and it taught me to trust my gut instincts. While I was away I decided I never wanted to go back into an office because I wanted to be free to do other things. Now I make the choices.'

TIPS
Finding a new direction

- Break home-based habits and routines by setting aside a non-working day – or at least an afternoon – every week on which you make a rule that you won't do any housework or admin.

- Don't tell everyone about plans that are dear to your heart while they are still in the early stages. Keep them quiet until you've got a concrete plan – and be careful who you confide in. There is always someone who will make you feel small if you don't follow through.

- Find your flow: look for activities that you enjoy for their own sake. Take inspiration from activities you enjoyed in the past – perhaps as a child – but gave up because other things got in the way.

- Making progress is implicit in flow, otherwise you get bored. Look for an activity that stretches your talents while not being so demanding that it makes you anxious.

- Keep an open mind: don't discount simple activities you might have dismissed five years ago.

Chapter 11

The Other People in Your Life

'It would have been the year Julian went up to Bristol.
George had felt this was the beginning of their time
together as a couple rather than as parents. It touched her
now to remember that he should have thought this an
event worth celebrating.'

Kiss and Kin by Angela Lambert

This chapter opens with the question all couples ask: will
my marriage survive? It also covers the particular issues
faced by single parents. Although single parents talk about
their experiences throughout the book, they face specific
issues which clearly deserve their own section. This chapter
– and this book – ends with friendship and support: no one
can survive the empty nest without them. One of the best
things about this stage is that parents have more time for
each other and for their friends.

Will your marriage survive?

This is crunch time for couples. Long before their children
leave home, parents start to worry about whether their
relationship will survive. The seismic shift of focus
away from the kids and back to your marriage brings
challenges, but it can also be hugely positive. Relationships mature and go through phases just as children do,

and this is potentially one of the most exciting growing phases.

It is no wonder, though, that couples panic about having nothing to talk about. For years children have been a common bond: the glue that binds the relationship together. And not always in a good way. Kids are also a convenient excuse to avoid doing things together or to swerve the discussion away from difficult subjects. There is always some child-related admin to distract parents from dealing with problems in their relationship or confronting uncomfortable truths. So the kids' departure not only leaves a gaping hole in the common ground between you but it also exposes the cracks in a partnership that their presence helped cover up. Many relationships don't survive such a massive shake-up. Divorce among the over-50s – now known as 'silver divorce' – has risen in recent years. Some parents see the crisis coming, having stuck with unhappy marriages until the kids leave. But couples with apparently solid relationships are often shocked to find the empty nest prompts uncomfortable questions about whether they want to stay together.

Case Study: Rob and Shona
Rob and his wife, Shona, had been happily married for over 20 years until the empty nest highlighted aspects of their relationship which had never been an issue before:

'When Bethany moved out and Dan went on his gap year I began to have very strong feelings of restlessness and dissatisfaction. I started wondering, *Is this what I really want?* I was very conscious of how separate Shona and I had become. I was wondering what there was between us to hold us together. It brewed for about six or seven months, and I think Shona would say that I was very cold during that period; I felt very cold inside. Suddenly, 23 years down the line we found ourselves asking, "Do I know you?", "Who are you?", "I know you're the person I have dinner with, but what do we really have in common?" We had the kids in common; that's been the focus of our attention. Now we still have the kids in common, but not in the same way. I think the kids leaving home has highlighted how Shona and I have been getting on with our own stuff and that we'd grown apart in the way that people do whose lives go on parallel lines and only interact about certain things. And, having recognised that, we've been trying to find some common ground again. It takes two: one of the members of the empty nest has to make a bit of an effort, and the other one has to be willing to participate.'

The new pressures on the partnership go far beyond the obvious loss of a common focus. The kids' departure often precipitates a wider sense of, 'Is that all there is?', a deeper questioning of what each person wants out of life. There may be a sudden realisation that this might or might not include your partner, and that in turn leads to a total reassessment of your relationship. It can be alarming to realise how much you've both changed since you had kids, and to discover that there's no going back to the way you were. Just as the birth of a baby changes a relationship overnight and requires huge adjustments and compromises, an adult child's absence prompts the same kind of shift, only in reverse.

Meanwhile, external pressures, such as the menopause, or redundancy, or the stress caused by ailing parents or friends, highlight issues in the partnership that have never been a big deal before. Many couples find that the gloves come off once there are no kids around; unconsciously in the past they might have avoided arguments in case it upset the children. Partners are now freer to say how they feel, and disagreements and annoyances are aired more openly. If it's equally balanced, this should feel like progress, but not if one partner feels got at.

In the midst of all this upheaval the prospect of re-inventing your relationship may feel daunting and exhausting. Yet research backs up an optimistic view of the impact of the empty nest. A study by the University of California, Berkeley, showed that marital satisfaction improves when the children leave. This contradicts the accepted wisdom that empty nest marriages flounder because couples have nothing left in common. The reasons are simple, according to one of the psychologists who led the research, Dr Sara Gorchoff. Speaking to the *New York Times* on 19 January 2009, she said, 'There are fewer interruptions and less stress when kids are out of the house. It wasn't that they spent more time with each other after the children moved out. It's the quality of time they spent with each other that improved.'

Nikki's experience with her husband, Marco, bears out these findings. Her son and daughter are now in their early thirties and left home when they were 20 and 18. She says,

'We all forget how bringing up children really tests you as a couple. Marco and I were quite young parents and I remember it being really tough, particularly in those early years and again when they were about 12 and 10. There were times when we were both so busy that there was not a lot of communication, it was just survival, and we grew quite far apart. Marco and I have grown a lot closer in the last couple of years; we've enjoyed each other's company more since the children left. You kind of indulge yourself more, you have the time to do what you want to do without having to consider other people, to travel. You can be more selfish I suppose.'

The most telling conclusion of the Californian research into empty nest marriage is that parents shouldn't wait until their kids have left to carve out more stress-free time together. Nor should parents wait to talk about their joint future. Implicit in the kids' departure is a clear choice to stay or leave, and this needs to be discussed. Making an active decision to continue with the relationship has to be a source of strength.

The first step towards getting the relationship on to a strong new footing is to acknowledge the new phase you are going through and that the relationship may need renegotiating. If you can discuss your assumptions and expectations for the future and the challenges it may bring, your relationship will grow stronger, and ultimately it will have a better chance of surviving the next big test for any couple: retirement.

'You can either just jog along and make the best of it or think of it as a new phase and decide how you both want it to be. And if you want different things, then actually you can separate,' says Philippa. A crisis in her marriage 18 months before her youngest child left home forced Philippa and her husband to consider seriously whether they wanted to stay together, and work on their relationship with the help of a marital therapist. It left them feeling much more confident about the future.

> 'At the time I didn't want us to break up because our son was still at home. So my immediate reaction to the crisis was whatever happens we won't break up right now, but we might break up when he goes. So we gave ourselves 18 months' breathing space in which to renew our relationship or not. In the end we did. We've got back what first brought us together – which was partly wanting to have children, but not just that. It was also a lot of shared interests and values and pleasure in doing things together. So, although the whole thing was a nightmare, it's made us more confident about the future without children than we might otherwise have been, because we had to decide whether we wanted to be together or not, in a very stark and dramatic way.'

While the ideal time for couples to start discussing their future and making plans is in the years before their kids leave, it is quite understandable if parents can't face it and firmly push the idea of a future without kids to the back of their minds. After 20-odd years of talking about the children it's all too easy for couples to get out of the habit of talking about their relationship; there's also the perennial excuse that there's neither the time nor the emotional space. Relate counsellor, Denise Knowles, confirms that 'Not many couples talk about their plans for their own lives. What tends to happen is that the focus is all on getting the children sorted, so parents may have a 10- or 15-year plan to get their kids financially through university, or get them all driving licences, but it's all geared towards getting the kids independent. What parents tend to ignore is that through all that process you are changing too. Your plans for your own future are not as concrete or as structured; you might have vague ideas about travelling when you retire, for example. And what you had thought you might enjoy doing in your fifties or early sixties may suddenly seem not so enjoyable.

'Acknowledging what is happening is a step in the right direction, talking about it together and even getting some outside help if the couple, or one of them, isn't coping. This is a big growing phase potentially for the relationship. If you can start to look at it as that and see it as an opportunity to evaluate what you've got between you and what you want in the future you can start to be quite creative about this period. It really is an exciting time, as long as both sides have maintained some kind of coupledom throughout their parenting phase. What's saddening is when couples don't realise that all they have become to each other is mum and dad.'

Different reactions to the empty nest

Tension can be triggered by differences in the way each partner reacts to the empty nest. If women take it hard, men struggle to sympathise. It's easy to misinterpret how the other person is feeling. Although women often think their husbands are heartless and hopeless at expressing their feelings about the kids' departure, the poor dears are often just trying to keep the atmosphere cheerful. Each parent is coping with loss in their own way, but at the same time they also have to deal with the fallout of what their partner is going through, and do their best to be supportive. Offering the right kind of support is not straightforward, and it's easy to get it wrong. It is a cliché that men are supportive in practical ways, while women are more verbal, but it's often true. And if one partner feels unsupported they may then go on to question what else is good in the relationship.

Of course, men feel sad, even bereft: one father I know spent the whole evening after dropping his eldest son at university weeping on his own. But mothers often feel their partners are putting too positive a spin on the whole thing, while fathers find it hard to get their heads round instinctive, maternal love and can't understand why women aren't so enthusiastic about launching the kids into the world. Mothers may wish their partners showed more emotion, while many men feel they don't have that luxury, because they feel responsible for holding things together. And when both sides are feeling vulnerable, it is all too easy to say the wrong thing.

Step-parents

It's even harder if one of the partners is not the parent. However understanding step-parents try to be, it's not easy to imagine what the other person is going through. One stepmother who moved in when her husband's three children were teenagers remembers some tense times when they first left home and used to drop in unexpectedly, which meant changing plans at the last minute. Although childless herself, she recognised how important it was for her husband to see his kids, and to continue supporting them. Even when she felt irritated she had no choice but to bite her lip, and she just trusted this phase would pass, as indeed it eventually did. However, accepting that your relationship has to take a back seat, even if for a brief period, demands that you have the patience of a saint.

The flipside of the situation is described by Jenni, a single mother whose partner moved in when her daughter was nine. She remembers,

'When Rhiannon went to university I missed her desperately for several months, but I didn't want to be too mopey about it because of my partner, who is not her dad and has no children of his own. He is very understanding about how I feel, and they have a good relationship, but he thinks I let her walk all over me. I think you're bound to get a bit of that if your partner isn't the dad. But it meant that I wasn't able to mourn because I had to pretend everything was fine because of him – I didn't want to make a meal of it.'

Dreams and expectations

Meanwhile, many men are disappointed that their partners are not as enthusiastic about the prospect of spending more time together as they had anticipated. The reality of the empty nest turns out to be rather different from the way they imagined it would be – at least in the early days. Relate counsellor, Denise Knowles, says, 'It's difficult if one partner is feeling, *Now is our time*, while the other is saying, "This is the worst time of my life." Immediately, there is a conflict of need or wish, and this often doesn't get acknowledged or noticed. The one who is gung-ho about the future may have gone along assuming that the other has the same expectations or wishes as they do, and it comes as quite a shock to realise that this isn't the case. And the partner who wants support can become quite resentful of the other person who wants to go out and enjoy life. There is a sense that the other person doesn't care as much about the children leaving home, which usually couldn't be further from the truth. Assumptions have been made because the couple haven't talked. And to start talking at this stage can be a bit difficult.'

What is more, men are understandably taken aback if they find that, after assuming that when the children left there would be more time to enjoy life as a couple, their partner is giving her all to her career. This is a relatively new element in the mix for recent generations of parents. After years of not being able to give work as much attention as they would like, many women are keen to invest more time and energy into it. This may be a source of conflict if the other partner is heading in the opposite direction and, after years with their nose to the grindstone, would prefer to kick back and explore life beyond work – ideally with a loving companion.

In fact, once the dust settles, this interesting role reversal suits many couples perfectly well. Each partner discovers a new side to themselves – and each other – as they seek fulfilment in a different area of life. Seen positively, it can stimulate a new direction for the relationship. Fathers see more of their departed kids, and may relish a more domestic role, while mothers enjoy their practical support as they explore a new identity outside the home.

However, sometimes good old-fashioned compromise feels like the only way forward. Julia, a lawyer, had been tempted to apply for another more demanding position when her youngest son left home after graduating, but ultimately decided to put her marriage first.

'Mike is more of a househusband since he gave up full-time work four years ago, so the children leaving has had more impact on him, although, as a man, I think he finds it easier

to accept them going away. He suggested I worked part-
time and, partly because I felt that I needed to spend more
time with him, I decided not to apply for the more senior
job I had been seriously considering. I've always wanted to
keep challenging and pushing myself. In the past I've seen
career choices as between a tight-fitting pair of stilettos and
a pair of comfy slippers, and I've usually gone for the
stilettos. But now I think maybe I will settle for the slippers
and see that there is more to life than work. We wanted a
joint project to focus on together, and in the end we bought
a ramshackle cottage. It took three years to do up, so it
was quite absorbing and it has helped to keep us together.
Of course, now it's done it's "What do we do next?" Mike
worries about it more than I do.'

Separate pursuits, common interests

In any marriage each partner needs to develop common
interests alongside independent pursuits, and this becomes
even more pressing once the kids leave. Maintaining a
balance between nurturing what you have in common while
developing your own stuff can be difficult. If both parents
work, the habit of boxing and coxing – taking turns to look
after the kids in the evenings and at weekends – may have
become ingrained. Couples often find they lead increasingly
separate lives in the years before the kids leave, which makes
it even harder to follow the experts' advice and make time
for yourselves as a couple.

Tom says,

'We've always done separate things. When you're bringing
up kids you have to, because one of you has to stay with
them. Lynn and I like each other very much, and we get on;
we have a lot of shared interests and a lot of shared views
about the world. But we have always had separate friends
as well. So now we have to sort of reconvene, to redefine

where we are as a couple. For over 20 years ours was a four-way relationship, and now it is a couple relationship again. That feels huge.

'Within my family set-up my responsibilities are now much more directed towards making sure not only that I'm making it through the transition OK but that Lynn is too. We need to make sure our relationship is strong enough to get through this. Because this is when people hit the rocks, if they run out of things to say to each other. But at the same time you have to maintain your independence and individuality. We keep saying we must go to the pictures and see friends more. Until you get into the swing of it you have to make yourself go out and do things to keep stimulated to make sure you are still there as a relationship. There are times when you've eaten dinner and you've talked for a bit. It used to be that that was your respite. You'd get through the day and that would be your time for relaxing, when the girls had gone to bed. But now it's, "What shall we do now?" I don't want to watch television, so I end up doing more work. Occasionally, we get the cards out or Scrabble. In a way you almost have to make yourself do that.'

It is important to be aware that breaking the habit of doing your own thing in order to invest more time in your relationship requires consideration for the other people in your life. Friends might be justified in taking umbrage if you are suddenly no longer available to them because you are always off with your partner. Besides, you may not want to do everything as a couple. It feels good to have separate friends, who like seeing you on your own and who you can confide in.

Find a joint project

A joint project helps bring partners together: decorating, giving the garden a revamp, playing music together or taking a course. Some people move house and get stuck into doing it up – which may bring back memories of their first home and early days together – others start dance classes. What matters is that you find something you both enjoy and are prepared to invest time and energy into. One partner may have to compromise and give the other the benefit of the doubt!

Case Study: Chloe

Chloe and Johnny, who are now based in England but spent most of their married life in developing countries, have ambitious plans.

'Recently, our daughter said, "You don't seem to have anything in common with Dad," and that is quite true. Johnny and I are very different people and we are a bit frustrated with each other at the moment. We are trying to find out what it is we do have in common, because we don't like the same books or hobbies or obvious things like that, although we do love doing DIY together.

'When you've been together for 25 years it's easy to take the connection between you for granted, and perhaps even get slightly bored with it. I think we need to celebrate it more. Rather than finding some hobby we could do together, what we really need is another big project abroad. So, when the children are settled, the plan is to go abroad again. We have lived a lot in crisis situations and we know how to handle our marriage at those times. If bombs are going off all around, you root for each other, you stop nitpicking. When there was fighting in Nepal I was just really glad when Johnny came home; I really didn't care whether he used the toothpaste correctly.'

Carving out time for yourselves

Couples will always be mum and dad at heart; their shared history as parents continues to be a core strength of the relationship. Increasingly, couples want to stay closely connected to their children's lives, but this demands yet another balancing act: how to carve out time together while devoting time and energy to the kids. It is natural for parents to talk to each other about their kids. Yet it can seem a bit backward-looking, and parents often feel that they should have moved on to other subjects. Tom says, 'We still find ourselves talking about the girls a lot and I think, *Why? They've got their own lives, why should we go on about their boyfriends or analyse their relationship with each other?* It's not my business any more. But then if you cut that out, what else is there?' Talking about your kids is a way of feeling close to them, and it is surely more acceptable to talk to your partner about them than to risk boring friends and colleagues. It's fine as long as it's only one part of your conversation: if your kids are the only thing you and your partner talk about, it's surely a sign that you need to find other things to interest you.

Although parents naturally want to help their kids, especially in a crisis, there may be times when their problems threaten to engulf your own relationship and hamper attempts to forge a new direction. Usually, these phases come and go, but there may come a time when parents need to assert their own needs. Janet says,

'At the beginning of this year we both started to feel we were getting too embroiled in our children's lives. It was difficult to narrow out a space for ourselves, because we were so busy responding to the kids' crises. Our son was having difficulties moving house, which meant a very stressful three months, and our daughter was made redundant and moved back home while she looked for another job. I was trying to be as supportive as I could, and so was Laurence. But we started saying that we need to step back a bit and let them get on with their own lives.'

The state of a partnership at the time the kids leave must be related to how things were before they came along: some couples live together for years before they have children, others no time at all. If it's a second marriage, the chances are that partners have only ever known each other as mum and dad: the relationship accommodated the children from the word go. The opportunity to see each other in a very different context can be both scary and exhilarating. Relate counsellor, Denise Knowles, was in this situation herself, having married her second husband when her son was a toddler: 'It can be a big worry for many people who have come into a relationship where there is already an established family, that they have only ever known each other with children. But the fact that throughout our marriage we have talked about this has kept us as a couple, and I think that is crucial. If the step-parent moves in when the children are older they might have gone into the relationship assuming the children will be leaving in a few years. You have to recognise that you may not have invested as much in those children, but your partner will have invested a whole lot more and therefore their loss will feel greater than yours. And you may have met your partner when he or she was a hands-on parent so you also have to adjust to the fact that they may be very different as a less hands-on parent. So it is something that is going to affect couples, but perhaps not in the way you imagined. And it's part of the deal if your partner is low and a bit depressed about the kids leaving; you bought into this. You need to think about how you can best be supportive while at the same time thinking about your own needs.'

You might think it would be easiest for couples who started their life together without kids for a few years: their early days surely offer reassurance that they can thrive again as a twosome. Hopefully, they have a degree of confidence that if their relationship was strong then, it can be again now that it's back to just two. But it feels so long ago that it can be hard to remember how things used to be and what you did with so much free time. These parents also face huge challenges in coming to terms with the way they have changed and acknowledging that there's no going back.

Of course, it's not always tough. There is a huge bonus in having more time together, and more privacy, and knowing that when you lock the door at night you don't have to worry about what time your teenager will make it home. Couples who have never known each other without kids often seize the new phase with relish: even small things make a big difference. Judy and her husband are both on their second marriages and have five children between them. She says,

'We are both enjoying aspects of the empty nest and the fact that this is the first time we've been together without children. I haven't been a grown-up like this since I was 21 and left my parents' home to get married – I'm now 64! Our youngest daughter was a vegetarian, so now we can shop very differently and prepare these lovely bistro-style meals. We sometimes have quiet candle-lit suppers, and at weekends we have breakfast together out on the terrace. It feels a bit like being on holiday – it's just very nice not having so many demands, and sometimes our house even feels like a hotel.'

Lack of desire

Living with teenage kids in homes with thin walls often puts couples off sex. So it's disconcerting if they find that, once that obstacle has gone and they could be bonking whenever they feel like it, they no longer really fancy it. Of course, it may partly be they've simply got out of the habit, but there are a range of factors that can inhibit desire. Feeling sad, or even just a bit lacklustre about life because your kids have left, can have a big impact on your mood in bed, while depression can affect desire because hormone levels get out of kilter. If the menopause coincides, it also challenges libido.

Added to this, you may be having second thoughts about your partner's physical appeal. The chances are that he or she isn't looking quite as hot as they used to. But get real: you've aged too. It could be that their grey hair and crows' feet are an uncomfortable reminder of your own age; there may be an urge to withdraw from the connection because it reflects on how you feel about yourself. Physical changes, which have gone relatively unnoticed for years, can strike like a thunderbolt when the kids go. While your children are still at home, the general liveliness of the household, as well as your involvement with the whole parenting bit, helps retain feelings of youthfulness. When they're not there you have to acknowledge your age and that you now look disconcertingly like the couples you see in over-50s adverts. It may not sit easily with the image of yourselves you hold dear.

If couples are concerned about the lack of desire, Denise Knowles, who is a sex therapist as well as a relationship counsellor with Relate, urges them to seek outside help. 'If there is a disorder of desire which goes on for more than about six months I would try to find out what that was all about. There are all sorts of emotions identified with the empty nest that have an impact on libido: depression, sadness, fear. If you have a partner who is not supportive of that, it creates difficulties. Alternatively, if you've got a partner who thinks thank goodness, because his erections are getting a bit weaker and he won't have to make so much use of them, a collusion gets set up. If lack of desire is bothering either one of you then it is important to get it checked out and do something about it.' (Details of Relate and other sources of help are listed at the end of the book.)

Deciding to part

The over-55s are less likely to seek outside help for relationship problems than younger couples. If they do, the issues that come up in counselling may take more time and harder work to resolve, simply because they are more ingrained. This could be one reason why so many couples call it a day when the kids leave. Yet, although the idea persists that it is easier on the children if unhappy couples wait to separate until they have left, it is increasingly challenged. Now the consensus is that parents need to acknowledge that their parting always affects the children, no matter what their age. Denise Knowles urges caution: 'One of the biggest mistakes that mums and dads can make is to think that now the children have left home and are independent, divorce isn't going to bother them in the way it would have when they were younger. It doesn't matter what age your children are when you decide to separate, it is going to have an impact on them. Just because they're older doesn't mean they are going to feel the loss and the change any less than when they were toddlers or adolescents. They may be more able to express themselves, which parents might not like. There are all sorts of different thoughts which go through children's minds. On top of everything else they might also feel guilty if they think mum or dad put up with being miserable and stayed together purely for their sake. So if you are going to separate at that point you have to make sure you are able to explain to the children that it isn't anything to do with them. It is a difficult and delicate thing.'

A young adult's view of divorce

Heidi's parents were in the process of splitting up when she went to university. When she arrived she became so anxious at the prospect of being away from her mother that she had little choice but to leave in the first term.

'It definitely was not the right time for me to go to university. Sometimes I think that if my parents had been happy and able to support me at that time I would have been a bit stronger and able to stay. But that wasn't the reality. It's a shame, because I think it would have been great. The woman at the counselling service was really supportive and under-standing; she didn't try to persuade me to stay, because she could see I would have found it very hard.

'I felt quite guilty for a long time afterwards, and disap-pointed in myself. I didn't really understand what was going on and how anxious I was and why. I thought I should be fine and that it was silly and I should just do it. I was quite angry as well. During my year out I had ten weeks of cogni-tive behavioural therapy, which really helped me overcome my anxiety. I then started at a university closer to home and it's fine; I'm much happier now.'

Apart from the considerable emotional turmoil, there are practical implications. These are familiar to all separated families, but loom larger when the kids are more independent. Whose home do they go back to in the vacations? Kids, no matter what their age, are still likely to take sides. And there may not be enough time to stay with both parents, because young adults' time is generally monopolised by their own preoccupations and peer group. For Linda's two children it is pretty straightforward. She says, 'This is their home. The kids always came back here in the holidays, never their dad's house, because he has a completely different life now, with young children. They never even stay the night there any more; that stopped when they went to university; it was a natural break.'

University counsellor, Ruth Caleb, sees many students whose parents have recently separated, and urges caution and consideration. 'Parents often wait to split up until the child is going to university. And if they get new partners they've got different things to do, new lives. That can be awful for the student if it's not handled thoughtfully; for example, if the family home is sold, how do they make the child feel they still have a home? You have to have a room for them, with all their things in it – or some means by which they know they've got a home.'

When Heidi's parents were divorcing, her mother moved into a small flat and, although her father still lived in the family house, Heidi, who by this stage had started at another university, was reluctant to go back. She gradually got used to not having a family base to go back to in the holidays and now lives in a shared student house:

'It was as though there was a massive dip: I was OK at home for years and then suddenly it was as if there was nothing. At the time I felt a bit lost and that created a lot of anxiety. Gradually, the family home became a more soulless place; I didn't want to go back there because it wasn't a happy place any more; it was that thing of not wanting to be somewhere because it would taint your good memories; I just wanted to forget about it. I stayed with my mother in her new flat once or twice but it felt uncomfortable and I realised she needed her own space. Now I feel more comfortable about not having a family base. I don't think this is something that is easy to adjust to, but I feel happy being independent from it now. It helps that I have older siblings who do have a stable family base and I can always go there. That makes it easier that I don't have a base with my parents. I'm lucky in that respect.'

TIPS
Marriage: changing your relationship

- Don't wait for the kids to leave to start doing more stuff together. Set aside time which is just for you: half an hour every evening, an outing once a week, a walk together at the weekend.
- Think about what you would do with more time together, and discuss it with your partner.
- Make a dream list of things you'd love to do over the

next ten years: anything from fabulous holidays to moving to the seaside. Then whittle it down to what's realistic, and work out ways of achieving it.

- Talk about how you'd like things to be in 10 or 20 years' time: where you would like to live, what you'd like to be doing.
- Resist the temptation to slump in front of the telly every evening. Get out the cards or do a crossword together.
- Root out some old tunes, get out the photo albums and have a good old reminisce – there's nothing like it to remind you why you got together in the first place.
- Separate interests are just as important as joint ones throughout the relationship, but even more important once the children have left.
- Come up with a joint project to work on together.

Single parents

Inevitably, single parents who live alone have a very different experience of the empty nest. From now on there is only yourself to think about, to cook and shop for; the need to compromise disappears and when you leave home you can guarantee that everything will be exactly as you left it when you get back. Many of the single parents I spoke to saw a clear advantage in facing the future with only themselves to please. They feel one step ahead of married contemporaries because they are already used to making an effort to be sociable, to build a life beyond children. They are used to spending time alone, particularly if their child regularly spends time with the other parent. They certainly don't envy contemporaries who find themselves facing up to the flaws in their relationship exposed by the children's departure. 'If I was in a relationship I don't think the empty nest would be any easier, ' Monica insists. 'At least I don't have to cook for anyone else or pretend things are the same. I've got no one to report to, I have a completely clean slate and I can do whatever I like.'

There are bound to be mixed emotions, however. As the saying goes, it's not having someone to do things with; it's having someone to do nothing with that you really miss. However gregarious and sociable you are, coming home to an empty house takes some getting used to. Often the relationship between single parent and child – particularly if there's only one child – is particularly close, with each side relying on the other for companionship and support. In larger families mutual dependence is watered down, less intense. University counsellor, Ruth Caleb, says, 'I have come across single parents with single children who know about each other's lives on a minute-to-minute basis. So when the child leaves it is really hard for parents not to have that sort of relationship any more, and I have seen several cases of single parents who are utterly bereft when their child leaves home. One or two have clung on, ringing up three or four times a day, and wanting the sort of contact they had when the child was still at home.'

Yet single parents get plenty of practice in being alone at weekends and holidays, if their child regularly spends time with the other parent.

Case Study: Monica

Monica, who has a very close relationship with her only daughter, Asha, felt ready to let her go, but that didn't stop her anxiety about a more permanent absence.

'Before Asha left, I had this huge fear of being lonely. But when she actually went one of the biggest realisations was that I had actually been lonely for years, ever since my marriage broke up. It wasn't Asha leaving that was going to make me lonely. And I had been using Asha as a sort of buffer against it. I then thought, *Actually, what I'm lonely about is the fact that I'm single, and I'd much rather be in a relationship.* I was actually lonely when she was here. The other thing her leaving brought home was that I had always looked forward to being with my man when I was older and my daughter had gone. I always had this image of Darby and Joan. With the man and the daughter gone it's just Joan.

'I miss Asha's support more than she misses mine. I find myself coming home from work and needing to talk to her, because in the past she would be there saying *that is not worth getting upset about.* She is very grounded and sensible and often says, "I think they've got a point, Mum, I think you're being a bit horrible." I miss that voice in my life. I can get quite worked up about people at the office and I realised how dependent I was on her to put me back on the straight and narrow. Now she has lots of people to support her and I don't. At first I soon realised I could just ring her up and say I'd had a terrible day. But I gradually stopped doing that, because I could see that it's not fair to burden her, and now I get over it myself. I'm very sensitive about not ever being the saddo needy mum. As a single parent I think you have to be really careful about that. I never ever want her to feel guilty about me, or dutiful.'

Starting a new relationship

All parents dread their kids feeling sorry for them; most of us have been there with our own parents as they get older. But it's a particular concern for single parents, whose kids are more likely to reflect on how mum or dad will cope without them. So when the kids leave it's often a wake-up call. People are finally inspired to make changes which may have been simmering away on the back burner for some time. Being single may be a perfectly happy state as long as there's someone you love to cook for, chat to and watch telly with. But without your child the prospect of the years stretching ahead without companionship strikes home and it makes many people realise how much they dislike the idea. Monica is already thinking outside the box:

'I know I don't want to live on my own, so I am actively looking at alternative ways of living with other people, and I want to instigate something in the next few years rather than waiting until I'm in my seventies. I live in an area where it was brilliant to bring up kids, but if I stayed here my life wouldn't change that much and I think that would be boring. It's a huge dilemma, because it will mean selling my house – Asha's home – and I think that will be a heavy blow to her. But I know that if I want to enjoy the next couple of decades, now is the time to start doing something about it.'

People who don't want to live alone could always take in a lodger or a student, but that's not for everyone. A pet helps, but it's not the same as a person and it's a huge commitment at a time when people need to seize their freedom. The most obvious solution is to set about finding a new partner; it helps that Internet dating has become a totally acceptable way of meeting people whether you're 55 or 25. When Anita's dog died shortly after her son and daughter had left, it inspired her to start dating for the first time in over 20 years.

'A dog is always there to welcome you home, always pleased to see you. My dog knew if I was upset and would come up and metaphorically put an arm round me. So when he died, the house really did feel totally empty. I started thinking that I had been single for so long, and I didn't particularly want to be, and I started thinking, Do I really want to be like this when I'm old? I actually started Internet dating. At the time I didn't think of it in terms of the kids leaving home but, looking back, it was definitely one of the reasons.

Initially, Internet dating felt like a big thing to do, but actually once you've done it it's no big deal. It just feels a bit strange, a bit upside down to the way you normally make relationships. But I don't think there's any harm in trying, even if I just end up making a few good friends along the way. I've seen a few people, one for quite a long time, and I went out with someone I'd met through friends. It didn't work out, and I found that very sad. But I haven't given up.'

Once the children have left, parents no longer need to worry quite so much about the effect that a new relationship could have on them. Both practical and emotional obstacles which might have deterred parents from looking for romance, consciously or subconsciously, vanish; for example, some parents feel uncomfortable about leaving their kids at night or for a weekend, but once they've gone, they are free to come and go as they please. What's even better is that your kids' reaction – approval, disapproval, embarrassment, silence – is no longer in your face. By the same token, the new person in your life doesn't have to bump into the kids at breakfast and has a chance to get beyond your parenting persona. Charlie found this liberating:

'Some gay men find it hard me being a dad, so it was easier once the girls had left. I never kept my relationships a secret, but I didn't want the girls to feel they would have to share me. After they left home I used to kid myself that I wasn't looking for someone, but that was really what I was doing. I used to tell myself I was going out to dance and have a good time but I was really looking for a partner. And then I met Robbie, who I'm living with now, and although he's 11 years my junior he settled me down. So I went back to a domestic life of a very different kind from the one I had with the girls. It's a new chapter in my life and I'm very happy with it.'

Parents often find that they have more emotional space for a relationship. When her two daughters were growing up, Nina had a boyfriend for 12 years, and although he didn't move in and they eventually separated, she now thinks it was one reason why her elder daughter preferred to spend the majority of her teenage years at her father's. When both girls moved into their own flats Nina took advantage of her new freedom.

'I immediately filled the gap left by my daughters with someone else. I had a fling with this guy who was about ten years younger than me for about a year, and he stayed in my flat on and off. I would never have had a relationship with him if the girls had still been at home, because they would have said, "What the hell are you doing?" He was a bit of a waif and stray. And indeed when my elder daughter came back unexpectedly from travelling she pointed out a few things about him that weren't great, and in the end we parted company.'

Holidays without children

Whether you are single or with a partner, holidays without the kids can take some getting used to. In theory the advantages are clear, and many parents have a long-established habit of taking regular weekend or longer breaks without the kids. Without the tyranny of school terms, you can go away pretty much when you want to, and take advantage of off-season deals. You can please yourself about where you go and who with, and the search for that perfect resort with something to keep everyone happy is finally over. You no longer have to think about taking a companion for your teenager and then spending every night worrying about them getting drunk or disappearing, or going off the rails.

But there are sad things too. Holidays trigger poignant memories of what you've lost and bring home the gap

between what life was like then and what it's like now. It's
a bit like Hallowe'en, Bonfire Night and nativity plays: they
will never be quite the same without your kids. Julia remembers the first holiday she and her husband took on their
own as a bit of a wake-up call:

> 'Because we were able to go outside school holidays it
> meant that there were all these other middle-aged couples.
> I remember looking around and thinking they all looked a
> bit elderly and then I thought, *Oh my God, that's us*. It
> made me feel elderly too because I no longer had children.
> That was actually quite horrible and it took some getting
> used to. But you do get used to it and you don't notice
> after a while. And you enjoy having that time and space
> to yourselves, and you get closer as a couple. But I still
> miss the outings and the picnics, and when I see parents
> having family days out with their children it makes me feel
> quite sad.'

It is impossible not to feel nostalgic about the bucket-and-
spade moments of the past, and many parents find July and
August particularly cruel months, because they used to be
such happy family times. Photographs preserve a rose-tinted
view of even the wettest, most bad-tempered, disastrous
holidays. I'm not sure how you get round this, although it
may help to think ahead, recognise that the summer months
could be difficult, and plan something to take your mind
off it.

Like most parents, Tom has mixed feelings about going
on holiday without the kids. He kicked off his life as a newly
redundant empty nester with an epic tour: four weeks with
his wife visiting old friends in Australia and South Africa
(she took her annual leave in one go) followed by two
months travelling around America on his own. He doesn't
sound entirely convinced when he says,

'We've had a couple of other holidays, just the two of us, and they've been . . . they've been brilliant, actually. But there are times when it feels very strange that it's just you, you haven't got the girls to focus on any more, to make sure they're all right, you don't have those big discussions about where you're going and you don't have to adapt what you're doing to suit them. There are no disagreements, and you almost miss that. The other thing I miss is that if you're travelling with kids people relate to you much more openly. Kids are a point of conversation, your key to meeting other people, understanding other people's cultures. Whereas, if it's just two middle-aged Brits on holiday, it's seen as something normal. That's what we never really wanted to be.'

As always, it helps to look forward not back: rather than continuing with the same kind of holidays you enjoyed as a family, seize the opportunities this break of routine offers. Time away from home gives a new perspective on life, the distance required to adjust to change and reassess your life. There is time and space to develop your relationship with your partner, or with a friend, to learn new skills, meet new people, or just relax (well deserved after years of childrearing). Make the most of not having the kids on board by doing the things you love and they hate. Now that you no longer need to compromise, you can book a holiday to a place you have always longed to visit but which the kids vetoed, or go on a course or a volunteer break they would turn up their noses at. And it's easier to stay with friends than it was when there were more of you.

Friends

When it comes to friendship and having a good time, we have a lot to learn from our children. What's the first thing they do when they come back from holiday? Phone their friends and rush round to see them. What do we do? Load the washing machine and pay bills. When the kids leave home it is easy to feel that fun, liveliness and spontaneity have gone with them and that parents have lost the habit of enjoyment for its own sake. But it is still there, in good conversation, having a laugh, dancing, parties, spending time with friends.

Friends are the best reminder that happiness does not depend solely on your children, and that you have a rich life – and, most importantly, a strong identity – outside the family. They are an endless source of shared enjoyment as well as an enduring source of support; they help make sense of what's happening in your life. And activities are often – although not always – more fun with an agreeable companion.

Yet, it is a sad fact of modern life that friendship comes way down the list of priorities for many busy parents. Family and work have to come first, and there's not much space for anything else. In this respect, single parents often have a head start. Couples can afford to be a bit lazy about friendship, because they can rely on a partner's support and companionship being there for them at home. Single parents can never take these things for granted, and recognise the need to be pro-active about getting out and seeing friends long before the empty nest hoves into view.

Anne says,

'Because I've been on my own since the kids were tiny I kept up a good social life. When the children went to their dad's, I made sure I went out and saw people, and as the children have got older I've been able to spend more and more time with my friends. My really good friends are a regular part of my life – and even though I now have a steady relationship with a man, it will never take the place of my friends. I know when I move they'll still come and visit me and I'll get to spend even more time with them. So I feel I've got everything. I don't worry about being lonely, because there is so much stuff I want to do – I just hope I've got the energy to do it.

If I miss cooking, which I love, I can be a Jewish mother for my friends. And I'm quite happy to take myself out to dinner with a book or a newspaper.'

Once the kids have gone, there should be enough time and energy to nurture new friends and breathe new life into old friendships, and perhaps reconnect with childless friends who drifted away during your most intense child-rearing years. There is time to remember birthdays, write chatty emails, return phone calls. Finally, after years of distracted conversations with the phone wedged into your ear while you do three things at once, there is time to talk properly.

Friendship and support

Good friends are a big help in getting through the empty nest, whether or not they have been through it themselves. Parents need support at different times and for different reasons, and partners can't always be relied on. Sometimes you need encouragement and confidence-boosting for new plans, at other times you just need a sympathetic ear and a shoulder to cry on.

However, friends who ring up eagerly expecting trauma and tears are not much help; they simply make you feel like pretending everything is fine and that you're coping brilliantly. It is more helpful to be given space to explain how you feel, which probably changes from one day to the next. The most thoughtful friends ring or send a casual text, perhaps about some unrelated matter. They might suggest an outing. This shows that they are there if you need them, or offers a way in to a conversation about how things are going.

Then there is the kind of dismissive support that is equally wide of the mark. Rose says,

'I knew that if I phoned up sobbing, people would say, "It's all right, he'll be back soon." And that is so not what I wanted; it totally misses the point. I didn't want anyone to stop me and tell me to cheer up, I wanted someone to say, "I've been in that place, I know how you feel."

'Yet some women I've met who do know how I feel, because they are going through the same thing, are too negative; they view the empty nest as the end of something rather than the beginning. I'm excited about the future as well as sad, and I want to be with parents who can acknowledge the loss but aren't stuck in their past and are going out in the world and moving on.'

Competitive parents

When it comes to big decisions about the future, experts advise women to be careful who they share their plans with, particularly if things are at an early stage. Critical friends may be too quick to pick you up on plans you haven't followed through, while partners may not be able to see beyond your familiar role. Meanwhile parents, bless them, never quite lose the habit of competitiveness. I naively assumed that it wouldn't persist past A levels, but of course it never really goes away. Parents still compare notes about their kids' careers, how often they visit, their jobs, marital status and finally their grandchildren. Charlie happily owns up to it himself:

'I think we are all quite competitive as parents really: you think, *Did I do as well as a parent as my friends did? Are our kids as happy, are they doing what we wanted them to?* It doesn't stop even when they have left the nest. I went through quite a difficult patch with one really close woman friend whose kids are similar ages to my daughters. I had a grandchild first, which was hard for her, and one of her children never left home, so she had something I kind of wanted – she didn't have a completely empty nest. But on the whole I got a lot of support and places to talk when I was missing the girls and that was very helpful.'

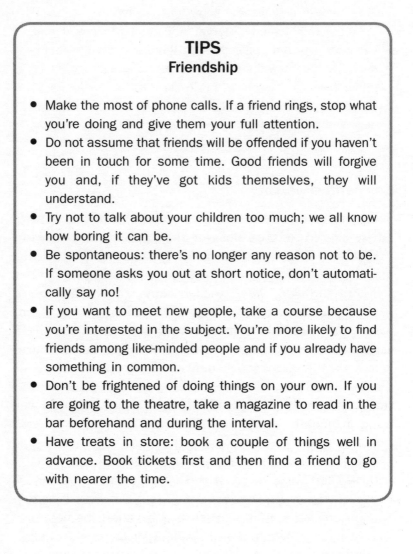

TIPS
Friendship

- Make the most of phone calls. If a friend rings, stop what you're doing and give them your full attention.
- Do not assume that friends will be offended if you haven't been in touch for some time. Good friends will forgive you and, if they've got kids themselves, they will understand.
- Try not to talk about your children too much; we all know how boring it can be.
- Be spontaneous: there's no longer any reason not to be. If someone asks you out at short notice, don't automatically say no!
- If you want to meet new people, take a course because you're interested in the subject. You're more likely to find friends among like-minded people and if you already have something in common.
- Don't be frightened of doing things on your own. If you are going to the theatre, take a magazine to read in the bar beforehand and during the interval.
- Have treats in store: book a couple of things well in advance. Book tickets first and then find a friend to go with nearer the time.

Conclusion

'Because she is no longer ashamed of how she lives, she has even allowed her parents to visit her . . . For three fraught days they commented endlessly on London's ethnic mix and the cost of a cup of tea, and although they didn't actually express their approval of her new lifestyle at least her mother no longer suggests that she come back to Leeds to work for the Gas Board. "Well done, Emmy," her father had whispered as she saw them onto the train at King's Cross, but well done for what? For finally living like a grown-up perhaps.'

One Day by David Nicholls

Before I embarked on this book I had little idea what a rich seam the empty nest would turn out to be. Certainly, I had a strong hunch that mothers and fathers are more deeply affected by their children leaving home than they often admit. This puzzling reticence seemed at odds with the times, where baring the soul is the norm and parenting is a hot topic. If bringing up kids gets so much attention, why ignore what is ultimately the whole point of parenting: launching them into the world?

As soon as I started interviewing parents it became clear how much there was to say and how raw emotions could be. This gave the lie to the idea that the empty nest went out with 1950s housewives and only affects mothers who need to get a life. In fact, the men and women who shared their experiences all had something new to say. One father who spoke to me early on taught me the first invaluable lesson. When I asked whether he had been upset when his daughter flew to Sydney, his reply put me gently in my place: 'No emotion is as straightforward as that.' One of the many things no one tells you about the empty nest is that it gives rise to a complicated, heady mix of emotions – it is certainly about much more than just feeling miserable.

No one mentions all the good stuff either, apart from glib references to getting the kids off your hands and vague notions of 'freedom'. This is partly because we have got stuck with an outdated idea of the empty nest that was true for our parents but is no longer the norm. Like family life gener-ally, the empty nest is constantly being reinvented. Unlike our mothers, who often found themselves totally redundant in midlife, we have more choice and a better chance of being able to pursue our dreams. There is no longer a sense of life turning camel-coloured at 50, with little to come in the future apart from retirement and grandchildren.

There is plenty of good stuff to look forward to, above all a continuing close connection with our adult children, something which was arguably not top of the agenda for previous generations. The empty nest is not the end of parenting, but rather a transition to a different kind of parenthood, which can be equally rewarding. The hindsight of parents like Nikki, whose son and daughter are both in their thirties, is illuminating.

Case Study: Nikki

Nikki's children left home to work when they were 20 and 18; her daughter now lives in France with her husband and daughter. She remembers,

'There was an enormous sense of emptiness when Lauren and Saul first left home. Even though I was working full-time

I missed them desperately at times; I still do. We still have very close conversations but the balance has shifted somehow. That's a good thing – it feels very positive. It's to do with them not needing us so much, and feeling that if something happened they would be OK.

'And it's different when you see them with their own home and their own family. The big change for me is that as they get older you're not responsible for their happiness any more, which is to do with coming to terms with the fact that they are now fully grown up. That was an immense relief; I worry less now because I realise I can't fix things. Of course if things go wrong for them I still get upset, and I feel sad with them. But in a way it's completely out of my control now, whereas when you're watching them taking those initial steps in the world you still feel responsible. Now, I am more of an observer.

'It's easy to get nostalgic, but I don't yearn for those years when we were bringing the children up. Recently I was going through the photo albums and thinking it was such fun – which it was, but it was also very hard at times. Life is good now, and I like the fact that the kids are getting on with their lives.'

In some respects the empty nest is a bit like childbirth: before the event it is impossible to imagine what life will be like on the other side. It looms ahead like an end in itself, a daunting hurdle which becomes the chief focus of attention, often at the expense of thinking about what comes next. It is only when parents are going through it that they can see that, like labour, the empty nest is merely the beginning of a whole new chapter which can be just as demanding and exciting as what has gone before. As time goes by, the significance of children leaving home gradually merges into the bigger picture.

One way to look at it is that when the kids leave home you ditch the rubbish side of parenting, as well as all the nice cosy stuff: the relentless routines, the anxiety, and the nagging sense of responsibility. And while the emptiness children leave behind feels bleak, it also allows the mind space to expand and to usher in a whole new array of possibilities. So, at the same time as they are dealing with the emotional upheaval of this massive transition, parents often experience a surge of energy and creativity which spurs them on to the next stage, to seize what the rest of life has to offer.

The parents who feel most positive about the empty nest all say the same thing: that they felt the time was right, either for their offspring to leave or to change tack themselves, or both. It wasn't that these parents were pleased to get the kids off their hands, or that they didn't miss them – far from it. Nikki says,

'I felt my daughter was ready to leave home from the age of about ten, and she went as soon as school finished – she took a diving job in Australia. My son was in a relationship and needed to have his own place. Them leaving just felt the right thing to do, and although it was sad there was a sense of relief that they had moved on to the next stage. Someone once said to me, "If your children go easily it means you've done your job as a parent." That's what it's all about, isn't it? You do your best to bring them up so they are rounded human beings and happy to go off into the world.'

Intellectually, of course, this makes perfect sense, but emotionally its truth can be hard to bear. It seems more like a cruel joke than a comfort that the ultimate reward for doing your best as a parent is that your children take off and leave, and it is this recurrent tug of war between head and heart that makes the empty nest – and indeed parenthood in general – so tough at times. But I hope the experiences of parents who feel ready to let their children to go, and to take off in a new direction themselves, inspire optimism rather than dissatisfaction. I admit that they give me a twinge of envy, even though they undoubtedly have their own struggles. But seven years into the empty nest myself I am beginning to feel that the time is right at last; some parents, myself included, simply take longer to get there. I can also see that progress is rarely straightforward, but that while there are highs and lows along the way, the overall trajectory is positive.

Resources

Useful websites and organisations

The Association for Family Therapy and Systemic Practice in the UK has details on its website about how to find a family therapist: www.aft.org.uk

The Association for University and College Counselling (AUCC) is an expert division of the British Association for Counselling and Psychotherapy. Find out more on www.bacp.co.uk/public

The College of Sexual and Relationship Therapists' website has a list of therapists in different parts of the country. See www.cosrt.org.uk

The Fatherhood Institute is the UK's fatherhood think-tank. See www.fatherhoodinstitute.org

Mumsnet has pages and forums for parents of teenagers and young adults. See www.mumsnet.com

Parentline is part of the Family Lives group of support providers. The website, www.familylives.org.uk, has forums for empty nesters, and a 24-hour helpline, tel.: 0808 800 2222. There is also a site for parents of teenagers: www.gotateenager.org.uk

Relate is the national provider of relationship and family counselling for people at any stage of their relationship or life, tel.: 0300 100 1234 or, to find out more about counselling face to face, online or on the telephone, visit the website www.relate.org.uk

Rona Cant For more details about the adventures of round-the-world yachtswoman, Rona Cant (Chapter 10), see www. ronacant.com

Student Counselling in UK Universities provides information about the support available to UK university students. It was set up by the heads of the various student counselling services, including the Association for University and College Counselling: www.student.counselling.co.uk

Students Against Depression offers information and resources at www.studentdepression.org

Australia

Australian Women Online is a news, business, career and lifestyle website for women in Australia and New Zealand. Visit www.australianwomenonline.com

Children, Youth and Women's Health Service has a website for parents in South Australia providing advice on living with adult children as well as on children leaving home. See www. cyh.com, or call the Parent helpline, tel.: 1300 364 100

Family Relationships Online provides families (together or separated) with advice about family relationship issues and information about government-funded services that can assist them to build better relationships. The website includes advice for parents and teenagers about handling change, and a guide on family separation for young adults. Visit www. familyrelationships.gov.au. The Family Relationship Advice Line, tel.: 1800 050 321, is a national service set up to assist families affected by relationship or separation issues.

Parenting WA is a telephone service that gives support on parenting to people living in Western Australia. It is available 24 hours a day, seven days a week, tel.: 1800 654 432. See www.communities.wa.gov.au

Parentline provides a confidential telephone service (tel.: 1300 30 1300) offering professional counselling and support for parents and carers of children in Queensland and the Northern Territory. See www.parentline.com.au

Relatewell (Family Relationships Institute Inc.) aims to provide opportunities for individuals, couples and families to achieve enhanced relationship skills at significant stages in life. The Institute also provides courses. Head Office: RELATEWELL Centre, 21 Bell Street, Coburg, VIC 3058, tel.: 03 9354 8854. See www.relatewell.org.au

Relationships Australia (RA) was originally known as the Marriage Guidance Council. RA offers a range of professional relationship support services and receives funding from the Australian Government through the Family Relationship Services Program. Visit www.relationships.com.au

New Zealand

Kiwi Families aims to provide practical advice and support for parents in New Zealand. It covers all stages and ages, from conception until children leave home, including tertiary education and helping your child find a job. Visit www.kiwifamilies.co.nz

Family Planning has a range of pamphlets and booklets about relationships, contraception and sexual health which can be downloaded. Hard copies can also be ordered via the website: www.familyplanning.org.nz. Alternatively, call the information line: 0800 4636 5463. Family Planning also

links to the website www.theword.org.nz, which is aimed
at young adults.

Relationship Services Whakawhanaungatanga is New Zealand's
largest counselling agency. It provides counselling and
education services to children, young people, couples
and families. Its website includes advice and information on
finding a counsellor: www.relate.org.nz

For students in Australia and New Zealand

All universities have counselling services which typically focus
on short-term counselling interventions and are characterised
by high levels of professionalism. **The Australian and New
Zealand Student Services Association Inc.** has a directory of
student services in different areas: www.anzssa.org

Further reading

Relationships

Terri Apter's books are essential reading for empty nest parents. They include:

The Myth of Maturity: What Teenagers Need from Parents to Become Adults, Norton & Co. (2001)

Secret Paths: Women in the New Midlife, Norton & Co. (1997)

You Don't Really Know Me: Why Mothers and Daughters Fight and How Both Can Win, Norton & Co. (2005)

Also:

Cecil Day-Lewis, the poem 'Walking Away', from the collection *The Gate and Other Poems* (1962), is also on the website www.cday-lewis.co.uk.

Kate Figes, *Couples: The Truth,* Virago (2010)

Simon Hoggart and Emily Monk, *Don't Tell Mum: Hairraising Messages Home from Gap-year Travellers*, Atlantic (2006) (for amusement!)

Andrew G. Marshall, *I Love You But I'm Not in Love With You*, Bloomsbury (2007)

Ruth Nemzoff, *Don't Bite Your Tongue: How to Foster Rewarding Relationships with Your Adult Children*, Macmillan (2008)

Susan Quilliam, *The Relate Guide to Staying Together,* Vermillion (2001)

Janet Reibstein, *The Best Kept Secret: Men and Women's Stories of Lasting Love*, Bloomsbury (2006)

Freedom

Mihaly Csikszentmihalyi, *Flow: The Psychology of Happiness: The Classic Work on How to Achieve Happiness*, Rider (2002)

Georgia Foster, *The Stress Less Mind* (a hypnotherapist and author specialising in breaking habits and building self-esteem), Georgia Foster (2009)

J. B. Priestley, *Delight*, Great Northern Books (2009)

Lillian B. Rubin, *Women of a Certain Age: The Midlife Search for Self*, Harper Collins (1979)

Elspeth Thompson, *The Wonderful Weekend Book: Reclaim Life's Simple Pleasures*, John Murray (2010)

The menopause

Michael Dooley and Sarah Stacey, *Your Change Your Choice: The Integrated Approach to Feeling and Looking Good Through the Menopause – And Beyond*, Mobius (2006)

Jenni Murray, *Is it Me, or is it Hot in Here? A Modern Woman's Guide to the Menopause*, Vermilion (2003)

For young adults and parents

The Family Planning Association publishes a range of booklets about sexual health and contraception, including 'Choose what you use: The FPA essential guide to contraception'. See www.fpa.org.uk.

Index